TABLE OF CONTEN

A HISTORY OF THE PUYALLUP TRIBE OF INDIANS

TABLE OF CONTENTS

Chapter 1 – Before the Settlers Came	Pg. 5
Chapter 2 – Explorers and Settlers Arrive	Pg. 23
Chapter 3 – Medicine Creek Treaty	Pg. 33
Chapter 4 – Education & Health/Families & Children	Pg. 69
Chapter 5 – Governmental Organization of the Tribe	Pg. 106
Chapter 6 – Fishing Rights Struggle	Pg. 115
Chapter 7 – Cascadia Takeover	Pg. 139
Chapter 8 – Tribal Law Enforcement	Pg. 160
Chapter 9 – Land Claims Settlement of 1988	Pg. 171
Chapter 10 – Self-Determination of the Tribe	Pg. 181
Chapter 11 – Financial Self-Determination/Casinos	Pg. 196
Chapter 12 – Tribal Organization Today	Pg. 203
Bibliography	Pg. 210

DEDICATION

To all our people, too numerous to name one by one, who have struggled for so many years; we dedicate this book.

We also dedicate this book to all those who have sacrificed immeasurably to uphold and sustain our tribal identity. We have survived against countless odds. Our people have made it possible for us to remain a visual and integral part of our homelands. This is our priceless heritage – our inheritance. From times past, we are the aboriginal caretakers committed to the concept of protecting Mother Earth with the rights to a separate identity, with all sovereign rights. We continue to claim our aboriginal ancestors' lands. Our inherent rights will pass from one generation to the next.

For this we are thankful.

CHAPTER 1

BEFORE THE SETTLERS CAME

In their aboriginal language the Puyallup Tribe of Indians are known as "S'Puyalupubsh," meaning "generous and welcoming behavior to all people (friends and strangers) who enter our lands." There are numerous variations on the spelling but the meaning remains the same. Leader of the Puyallup Nation Henry Sicade (1866-1938) once wrote: "[T]he Puyallups got their name from the Plains people because they were quite generous and gave more than was needed."

Before the coming of settlers from Europe, the Tribe lived unfettered, inland on higher grounds along the southern portion of Puget Sound, situated centrally on the Pacific coast. Today many Tribal members continue to make their homes there, generally near the Puyallup River and around Commencement Bay in Tacoma. Back in the times when Indians were free to live their lives without interference, the Puyallup Tribe was keenly aware of the wealth in natural resources with which they were blessed, and saw themselves as stewards of the land responsible for existing in harmony with every other living thing. The Tribal members live by this responsibility to this day, and have contributed immeasurable efforts to preserve what remains of the earth's gifts to humankind.

Before the English language was forced upon the Tribal people, the Puyallups spoke the same stock language as the rest of the Salishan family of tribes that once thrived in the Pacific Northwest. There were many dialects spoken, and the Puyallup's is known as "Twulshootseed." Salishan is taken from the term "Salish," which is used to name all the various tribes that made up the original peoples of the Northwest coast – the Nisqually, Squaxin and other Salishan tribes. The tribes distinguished themselves according to the environment in which they lived and developed cultural differences. There were river people, saltwater people, inland people and prairie people. With no battles over land ownership to set up boundaries of privately held property, the various tribes traveled about at will.

Many of the Salishan tribes are intimately related by marriage, and such kinship extended over the mountains into Eastern Washington. In fact, young Puyallup men have always been welcome and encouraged to marry outside of their Tribe. In the days of their ancestors, this helped ensure close diplomatic relations among tribes and made for expanded hunting and fishing grounds for families. Marriages between members of two different tribes whose villages were a great distance from one another brought increased social standing to the families involved. Parents would arrange such marriages with the consent of tribal leaders while the children were young. Once the children were of age, the marriage ceremony was held that included an exchange of property between the families. The groom's family would give the bride's kin gifts of higher value than the bride's family gave them. Either the bride would leave her village and tribe, or the groom would, depending upon agreements made between parents and tribal leadership.

Marriages within adjoining tribal villages were much more common and were usually not arranged like long distance intertribal unions. Rather, boys and girls would grow to marrying age and could choose their own mates although it was up to the parents whether the union would or should take place. These marriage ceremonies were the same as for the arranged marriages, with the presentation of gifts and happy family reunion gatherings at the birth of the first child.

Infants were made to feel warm and safe by wrapping them tightly in blankets such that movement was completely restricted. Babies fell quickly to sleep this way. Secured snugly to cradleboards, babies would spend hours in this manner both awake and resting near their attentive mothers. Part of raising an infant properly included shaping the youngster's head. In Puyallup tradition, a head gently formed into a certain shape was seen as a sign of beauty. To achieve the desired shape a square piece of cedar plank would be attached at a downward angle at the top of the cradleboard and the child's head would be tucked underneath the piece to gradually flatten the back of the head and the forehead.

As they grew, both boys and girls were given strict training by one or more men in the tribe designated to do so. These trainers, and the children's parents, made sure the child was raised according to traditional Indian ways to ensure a better future life for the child and better social standing for the family and village.

Boys entering puberty would embark upon "vision" or

"power" quests that took them away from their village to a distant lake or stream where they would fast and bathe ritualistically. A girl's first menstruation would mark her step into womanhood at which time she would move into an isolated hut near the village where she would fast and bathe. She was obligated to neither look at nor speak to anyone for up to ten days.

While the Coast Salish tribes held their own unique ways and values, they were all connected in one way or another by commonalities in religious observances, myths and traditions. Historians and archeologists confirm that the early Puyallups were deeply spiritual people, and spirituality continues to be a key element among the generations to this day. The Tribe's forebears observed high reverence for a great creator and respected the spirit that they believed possesses every living thing. The same is true today, as the immigrants from overseas that laid waste to the Puyallups' earth-centered way of life centuries ago failed to extinguish the fervent, unifying spirit that burns in the tribal heart of every Puyallup.

That nameless and untouchable bond of spiritual connectedness reaches beyond life and into death for the Puyallups. While death was, of course, a solemn occasion for the Tribe, it was also one in which the spirits of their ancestors seemed most alive and ready to offer a gentle hand, bringing with it a sense of reverent, profound joy to the living. The loved one who had passed away would be laid to rest in one of two ways. Inland villagers would bury the body in the ground and construct a peaked shelter of cedar planks to protect the grave. Villagers closer to salt water would wrap the body in robes and blankets and place it in a fishing canoe suspended high in the trees. In either case, property of the deceased was placed with the body and included practical items such as bows and arrows, a saddle, and eating utensils, along with more personal belongings. Mourning was relatively brief and viewed as a time for re-purification of the bereaved's spirit. For instance, a surviving spouse would combine sweats with cold water plunges to cleanse away remnant smells and other imprints of the deceased.

For centuries the Puyallup People made their homes in the shadow of Mount Tacobet (or the anglicized name Mount Tacoma), today known as Mount Rainier. The great mountain feeds the Nisqually and Puyallup rivers, their creeks and tributaries that flow all the way to the shores of Puget Sound. These waters teeming with life provided everything the aboriginal peoples needed including communication routes for canoes to travel, which allowed for tribes to mix and get to know each other. Living on the flat and calm waters of Puget Sound, the Indians of the region became masters of the canoe. In fact, the Puyallups considered canoes to be the most important possession and upon the death of the owner his canoe would stay with the family blood line. To fish at night, a fire would be built in the bottom of the canoe to illuminate the water: fish could be speared or netted. A variety of different canoes were built and used by Indians on Puget Sound, some large enough to carry dozens of people: war canoes, freight canoes, trolling canoes, shovel-nosed canoes, one-man canoes and children's canoes.

John (Xot) Hote, one of the signers of the Medicine Creek Treaty representing the Puyallup Tribe of Indians, left some words for his people regarding the waters, its salmon, and the revered mountain. "Tacobet fed them and her other grandchildren, the Yakimas, through her rivers, the Puyallup and the Yakima, which she kept always supplied with life-giving fish and clear, cold water." According to stories Hote's forefathers told him, Tacobet received this privilege from Guilbitch, the moon. They said that in the beginning of things Tacobet was a lovely woman. She was less powerful only than the moon, which gave her the privilege of choosing what she would like to be when the end came. She wished to be a mountain, she said, because in this way she might always feed her grandchildren, sending everlasting life to her own people, the Puyallups.

With the waters flowing from Mount Rainier feeding the rivers and streams, the land grew thick with fir, spruce, alder, vine maple, cedar and cottonwood trees, lush ferns and soft mosses, thick grasses and a multitude of wildflower varieties. The heavy seasonal rainfalls that typify the Northwest climate also contributed to the People's more than ample food supply. They were fed by both the land and sea: salmon, shellfish, wild game, roots, nuts and berries made for a diet rich in all the nutrients they needed. The environment was resplendent in the wealth of natural resources, providing for all the Tribe's needs and allowing the people to live healthy, happy lives. There were no worries of where the next meal would come from, and the Tribe enjoyed the freedom to practice their religion, train their children and take care of their elders according to traditions reaching back millennia. "When the tides were out, the table was spread," is often repeated by tribal historians. The Puyallups were – and still are – supremely aware of the blessings of the earth that were all around them. From their earliest days the People saw themselves as stewards of the Creator's gifts, taking great care to respect all living things rather than exercising dominion over them as is the white man's way.

On land the towering Western red cedar tree provided homes, utensils, clothing, canoes for transportation, saddles for horses, and wood to make fires and cook meals. The Puyallups built and lived in permanent cedar longhouses clustered in villages that were scattered throughout the rich country of the Puyallup river valley and beyond.

The village was the heart of the Tribe, and villages were situated either at the juncture of two streams or at the mouth of a stream where it entered the Sound. Each longhouse held four to six families bound by blood or marriage, but not exclusively. Each village was self-sufficient, supplying their own needs with special care being given to the elders who were closely attended to and watched over by everyone.

Social organization within the Tribe placed men in the lead. Within the male population, technical expertise in hunting, harpooning and canoe building, as examples, set individuals apart and attracted them much respect. These men were seen as types of authority figures for they possessed skills and natural talents that took much time to learn and develop. Their knowledge and proficiency were valued highly and brought the men high social standing.

Men who excelled in human affairs were the leaders and chiefs of the village. They strived for peace among their people, and as diplomats would help settle quarrels and make decisions by which the entire Tribe would have to abide. A third type of authority was the warriors of the Tribe. With their finely crafted weapons they welcomed a fight and stories of their bravery ran deeply among the people. Warriors would act as both protectors of the villages and aggressors who would lead raids for profit. Should conflicts between tribal members fail to be settled by peaceful means, the warrior would step in and take control of settling the disputes.

At gathering times, a tribal member, generally an esteemed man rich in material goods, would invite certain tribal members and guests from other tribes to a potlatch. During these bustling, eventful social happenings, invited guests would arrive by canoe and bring considerable gifts to the host. Keeping canoes abreast, the leader or warrior of the visiting groups started a power song and the others would join in. Tribal members of a higher class would give more than the others, a display of wealth to gain prestige by showing that giving a large amount of goods wouldn't impoverish the giver. After all the guests had arrived, their gifts were given and the host would in turn distribute valuable items in great give-aways to those whom he designated. Marriages would be arranged and consummated, delicious feasts enticed every appetite, and games of sport and skill were held whereby scores between feuding individuals could be settled without serious physical harm.

The Western cedar also provided the Tribe with raw materials to make their own canoes, a cornerstone to the Tribe's way of life. Fallen trees were used whenever they were found. To fell trees, a combination of hacking at the trunk, burning it and driving in wedges successfully brought them down. No parts of the tree went to waste. Strips of supple cedar bark were made into everyday clothing and for other occasions – shawls and robes were worn in winter to give protection from the chilly, damp elements.

The Puyallups were known to be, and still are, consummate weavers. Their expertly made cedar bark baskets, and those made using other native plant species, were considered valuable trade items. Puyallup women excelled in weaving, particularly baskets. Baskets were made in a wide range of styles to accommodate a variety of uses. Coiling and twining (wickerwork) methods were used. Coiling made baskets water tight. These were weaved so finely that they held water without losing a drop, making the perfect pot to cook in. Large stones heated in the fire could be placed in these baskets to bring water to a boil. Loosely weaved twining allows air and water to pass through. This method of weaving was used to create sieves for fishing or containers in which to dry or store foods. Baskets were worn around the neck when berry picking so that both hands would be free.

Every tribal member had their own collection of plaited mats in various sizes and thicknesses for sleeping and sitting. They made strings of many types by twisting thread-like fibers of barks and grasses. Puyallup women were prolific knitters, making their own yarns from animal furs. Plant materials were used in most ingenious ways. For example, cottony cattail fibers made for softer headbands when toting filled baskets in this manner.

The Puyallups' weaving skills attracted the attention of other tribes like the Yakama who traveled from the arid regions of Eastern Washington to barter with their Puyallup neighbors. Individual Puyallup tribal members owned personal property and could amass considerable wealth if that be their fate. Trading within the Tribe was continuous. Services (say, from a shaman or healer) were paid for in goods. Gifts were often given between tribal members and families with no reciprocation desired. Property was distributed upon all ceremonial occasions, particularly the potlatch.

To both maintain bodily cleanliness and attain spiritual refreshment on a personal or communal level, the Puyallup People utilized small sweat houses made of vine maple limbs and cedar. Generally located away from village sites, sweat houses were built to shelter one man or woman as the case may be. The concept was the same for the larger and permanent communal sweat lodges that were dug into the sides of hills. These

A large collection of baskets owned by William and Alice Blackwell, arranged on display outside their Tacoma residence, ca. 1900-1913. An older woman (possibly Alice Blackwell) stands behind the basket display. These baskets exemplify the high level of craftsmanship the Puyallups developed to make baskets used for cooking, drying foods, storage and a host of other uses. Courtesy of the Washington State Historical Society.

would hold up to six men or women at a time. To make a sweat, pouring water on hot rocks inside the lodge would send up billowing clouds of steam to purify the body and soul. Men would often compete to see who could stand the heat the longest and therefore be deemed "toughest" by his peers. Participating in sweats was entirely a matter of personal choice; it was neither expected nor compulsory.

Salmon, native to the Northwest and once swimming in great abundance, are sacred to the Puyallup people and an object of veneration. For the Puyallups and other aboriginal peoples of the Northwest coast, fishing for salmon was a way of life, and livelihood. Providing a constant supply of good eating for every tribal member, it is said that the salmon were once in such abundance they jumped right into the canoes. Salmon formed the basis of the aboriginal economy and was a major commodity for trade with other tribes. The people offered much respect to the salmon and even though tribal fishermen brought in extraordinary harvests, in return the people were blessed with the continuation of returning runs year after year. Methods of fishing were elaborate and highly effective and included the tripod fish trap, nets, spearing, and still fishing.

Illustrating the importance of salmon to the Puyallup Tribe, an annual "first fish ceremony" was held when the first salmon was caught each spring. Every tribal member ate from this chosen fish, as all the people gathered for this joyful cultural festival and religious ceremony that included singing and dancing in traditional ritual and regalia. To help ensure the return of the salmon in abundance the next year, the intact skeleton of this first fish would be returned to where it was captured, positioned so that it was heading upstream.

The formal honor of catching the big fish was bestowed upon

selected tribal men. Women, with help from the children, were charged with cleaning the fish and preparing them for broiling, smoking or drying. Women also brought in smaller and more easily caught seafood. Digging for clams and shellfish happened often at night during low tide when the moon was full and bright. This simple example illustrates how the delineation of chores among the People was not black and white according to gender. Each knew pretty much how to do the others' task, although precise technical skills were often kept separate. Men did the hunting on land, sometimes traveling long distances on highly organized hunts involving learned skills passed down for centuries. Hunting was not always done in groups. Oftentimes men would strike out on their own within a reasonable distance of home, maybe taking with them a young man in need of training. Weapons of choice ranged from bows and arrows, spears, spring nooses and snares, to simpler implements like clubs and rocks.

The People enjoyed deer, elk, water fowl and birds, and other wildlife big and small. Meat was preserved by smoking it in dome-shaped structures made of boughs built over smoldering cedarwood fires. Horns were carved into tools and utensils. Furs and tanned skins were crafted into shirts, leggings, skirts, dresses, footwear, blankets, overcoats, riding gear for horses, and ceremonial regalia intricately embroidered with beads and shells. Furs were worn in colder months for warmth and protection from seasonal rains. Ducks and other fowl offered not only meat rich in fat, but feathers needed for all types of daily and ceremonial uses.

The duty of gathering foods inland was in the hands of the women, girls, and little children of the Tribe, although men, too, picked up earthy delicacies on their outings. Roots were dug in the springtime when they freshly sprouted, and only the best tasting were chosen.

The Puyallups were masters at woodcarving and created intricate and meaningful artistic designs considered as some of the finest authentic aboriginal art in North America. These skills were passed down through generations of families and today master carvers in the Puyallup Tribe keep the ancient craft and its deep meaning strong among the people.

It wasn't all work and no play for the Puyallup Tribe, as the People participated in all sorts of games, sports, and contests between villages. Winning meant not only greater social standing; these types of competitions allowed personal antagonisms and grievances between tribal members to be settled. Male village leaders, and young men seeking to establish themselves as being capable of leadership, often competed against each other to gain superiority and to impress other tribal members with public shows of physical and mental prowess.

Contests of physical skill and strength, such as wrestling and archery, were sometimes more openly hostile and aggressive than games, which were made thrilling by high-stakes bets of personal wealth. Sports were played for the pure fun of it and the People thoroughly enjoyed good-natured pastimes like swimming and mock war battles.

Contest challenges could be asserted by one Puyallup to another or with neighboring tribes as well. Once any type of challenge was delivered it was taken quite seriously. If the challenger won, he had full right to seize absolute power and control over the loser including life and death, his wife, his slaves, and all personal possessions. If the man being challenged won he could exact some sort of extra revenge on his vanquished foe, but prestige could be gained were he not to do so. Exhibiting not only strength and agility but higher character traits like compassion and sound moral judgment made for an even greater victory for the winner and sure admiration from his fellow People.

Gambling is an ancient practice among the Puyallups, and was often used in place of physical aggression to address everything from mere squabbles to more serious issues. One of the most important games was the disc gamble, which could be played simply or on a much grander ceremonial scale that involved participation from every man and woman in the villages. The disc gamble was, very basically speaking, based on the concept of the modern shell game in which one must correctly decide under which shell a ball is hidden. The rules of the bone gamble, popular among the Puyallups and other tribes all the way up into British Columbia, Canada, were much more complicated. Groups of men and sometimes co-ed teams of about 15 players on each side would participate. Much singing and ceremony accompanied this occasion. Women had their own game to play—the beaver tooth game—also known as the dice game because it was akin to tossed-dice games played today except that the women used marked beaver's teeth.

Whether at work or play, the Puyallup Tribe enjoyed life to the fullest. Every day presented opportunities of something meaningful to do not just for survival and the continuation of the tribal lineage, but also for sheer enjoyment and pleasure. The concept of time and the cycles of life and death revolved around the seasons and the existence of natural occurrences, as the tribal members were keenly in tune with the earth's cyclical patterns. The night sky and the sun, the snows and blooming of wildflowers, and the return of the salmon all helped shaped the Native people's reality, permeating every fiber of their being. Like the cedar tree, the men, women, and children of the Puyallup Tribe were rooted in the earth's soil forever. They, too, raised their arms to the sky like the strong cedar branches, and expressed humble gratitude for the benevolent forces that blessed them with such bounty. When the winds blew and the great trees swayed under its force, so, too, did the children of the earth below, bending in respect to the power of the wind and absorbing wisdom of the ancients in its whispers.

*   *   *

While the preceding pages provide only a thumbnail description of the complex social and political structures of the Puyallup Tribe, for the people this was the culture they were born into, and which they saw systematically eradicated in a very short period of time. As soon as immigrants began filling the Northwest from land and sea, a catastrophic ripple effect took hold throughout the Puyallup Tribe, causing great suffering for every one of its members. It wasn't long before degradation to the environment took its toll on the natural resources once so plentiful in the Great Northwest. Fish species began to die out, salmon stopped returning to their spawning ground, trees were cut down with abandon, rivers were dammed, and ecosystems were destroyed.

When navigators and traders first arrived at Pacific coastlines and into the Strait of Juan De Fuca that leads into Puget Sound, they eyed the aboriginal peoples with a mixture of inquisitiveness and trepidation. The Native peoples reacted likewise to them. Spanish exploration expeditions and British forays into the New World for trade opportunities made for brief encounters with the Indians of Puget Sound. Missionaries, fur traders, and fortune finders sometimes clashed with the Native peoples and other times were seen as more of a curiosity than a direct threat.

Soon Europeans in greater numbers filled the lands. With the coming of these foreign immigrants from across the oceans, aboriginal peoples of the Pacific Northwest coast found themselves with no choice but to acquiesce to the onslaught of settlers that took up their homes on Indian land with or without cooperation from the Native peoples. Even though the Puyallups remained generally peaceful while their harbors filled with odd-looking ships that seemed to carry an uncountable number of strange, new faces, the welcoming Natives were pushed aside onto reservations and left to fend for themselves while their caucasian counterparts fed heartily on the cornucopia of the New World.

Time would soon reveal the insidious intent of the new arrivals to America, and the Indians, along with their way of life, would be changed forever. Spreading disease, outright exploitation, and thieving trickery well describe the methods white men used to get what they wanted from the Indians. Early on the Native peoples, including many Puyallups, united and fought back in sporadic wars, but they became too outnumbered by the newcomers. Decades later in the 1960s, when Indians across the country galvanized to regain what had been stolen from them, the Puyallup Tribe was right in the thick of things in their quest to take back what was theirs, including many acres of land and their rights to fish in their homeland's waters. The People proved to be formidable adversaries against those who would deny them what their ancestors held as sacred, and the fight continues to this day.

ORIGIN OF FIRE

All the fire in existence was formerly in the possession of two wrinkled old hags who would neither sell, loan, nor give it away. They were deaf to all blandishments or threats. Do what he might, no Indian could get any fire. Coyote, one of the chief deities, was besought by the people to do something to help them to obtain fire, for they were cold and needed cooked food. After much thought, Coyote worked out a plan. He expected a hard struggle and a big race and so he stationed various animals out in a line reaching from the old grannies' abode to the animal peoples' country. The strongest and best runners he put on the stations nearest the old hags and tapered off with the weaker. Coyote appointed a man to secrete himself near the old women's lodge and instructed him that at a given signal he would attack them. Everything being arranged, Coyote went up to the hut, complaining of cold and begging permission to go in and warm himself. The old hags, suspecting nothing wrong, permitted him to enter their wigwam. All at once the concealed man jumped up and rushed at the women. During the fighting and scratching that followed, Coyote seized a firebrand and rushed off toward the Indian camps. The old hags, seeing their fire going, struck out after Coyote, pressing him hard. With lolling tongue and panting breath he came up to the panther, who took the brand and went on with it. Just as he was about to give out, the bear relieved him and carried it on to another animal, and so the brand passed from one to another, the old hags all the while closely pursuing, trying to recover their stolen fire. Luckily the firebrand passed safely along the line until it fell to the poor, little, squatty frog. By this time there was not much left of the brand and froggy was never much noted as a runner. With his slow and labored hopping, the old women overtook him. It was no use trying to run further, as he was going to be caught. Just then he swallowed the fire and jumped into the river, going to the bottom with the coveted fire in his belly. Between the racing and the fire, it had gone hard with the frog for he had lost the tail of his youth and was but a stumpy representative of this former self. He came up, however, and spat the fire out upon some pieces of wood. Consequently the Indians have ever since had fire, for it remained in the wood and they could extract it by rubbing or twirling.

Excerpted from Robert Montgomery's
History of the Puyallup

CHAPTER 2

EXPLORERS AND SETTLERS ARRIVE

In the late 1700s, Spanish and British explorers traveled up and down the Pacific Coast of North America searching for the fabled Northwest Passage, a waterway connection between the Pacific and Atlantic oceans. Such a passage would provide an enormous military advantage—not to mention economic opportunities—to the country that located it.

In 1774, Spaniard Juan Perez sailed from Mexico with a crew of mostly Mexican sailors, and became the first European to discover and explore the coast of Washington state. Perez's expedition visited Nootka Sound and made land on Vancouver Island, naming it San Lorenzo. The expedition also sighted the Strait of Juan de Fuca, but did not venture further inland. The following year, an expedition led by Bruno de Heceta anchored off the coast of Washington, near what likely was the Moclips River. A party that made land was killed by Quinault Indians.

Captain James Cook was the first Briton to explore the

Northwest. In 1778, he anchored in Nootka Sound, where he traded with local Indians. Bad weather prevented him from entering the Strait of Juan de Fuca. Although Cook did not venture far into Washington state, he played a key role in promoting future exploration. In 1784, he published "Voyages to the North Pacific Ocean," in which he described the lucrative sea otter pelt trade. Following the book's publication, many individuals from many nations rushed to enter the fur trade.

Although Cook's book inspired entrepreneurs to venture to the Pacific Coast, it wasn't until twelve years after Cook's voyage to Nootka Sound that another expedition would sight the Strait of Juan de Fuca. In 1790, the Spanish Manuel Quimper expedition spent two months exploring the north and south coasts of the strait. Quimper reported several encounters with Indians, noting in many cases the high degree of cooperation and communication the explorers met.

A short two years later, Puyallup tribal members would come face to face with the first European explorers in Puget Sound. In December 1790, Captain George Vancouver of Britain was given command of the Discovery in order to explore the North Pacific Ocean. The purpose of Vancouver's mission was to arrange diplomatic talks with Spanish representatives in Nootka Sound, and also to continue the search for the Northwest Passage.

In April 1792, Vancouver's expedition entered the Strait of Juan de Fuca. On May 19, the crew anchored between Bainbridge and Blake Islands. Vancouver made careful note of all the natural features in the area, and named each one of them, including visible peaks and islands. Mt. Rainier, for example, was named for Vancouver's friend, Rear Admiral Peter Rainier. Vashon Island was named for Captain James Vashon. He named the northern area of what is now Puget Sound Admiralty Inlet.

Only the area south of Tacoma was named Puget's Sound after his lieutenant, Peter Puget.

Puget and a small group of men were given orders to spend a week exploring Puget's Sound and to make a detailed report. In the predawn hours of May 20, 1792, Puget's crew set out down the eastern shore of south Puget Sound. In the Colvos Passage, just north of the Tacoma Narrows, Puget's crew noticed they were being followed by Indians paddling along the western shore in a dugout canoe. When the Indians went ashore, Puget's crew followed and left beads and trinkets in their canoe as a token of friendliness.

Puget's party encountered Indians once again while paddling in Wollochet Bay, where they noticed a village and women and children digging clams on the beach. The digging party quickly left the shore, but men returned. Puget's party gave the Indians gifts to show their intentions, and were invited by the Indians to land.

When the explorers set out again, several Indians followed behind in canoes. That night, while Puget's men made camp on Green Point, the Indians watched from the water.

Although the first encounter with what were likely Puyallup or Nisqually Indians was peaceful and pleasant, an encounter the following day proved to be a little more tense. Puget's crew began approaching a village on shore but stopped when Indians in a canoe indicated for the party to leave. Puget's party did so, but not before tying copper and trinkets into a piece of wood, which they left floating in the water for the Indians to pick up. The Indian canoe party did so, and then ventured alongside Puget's party. Puget noted in his journal that two of the three men in the canoe were missing eyes and were marked with smallpox pock marks, indicating that the effects of European explorers had still managed to reach them.

Eventually, other canoes arrived with nearly 20 additional people. Puget's party stopped in the early afternoon to eat. They found a couple of small creeks entering the sound and put a fishing net across to catch their afternoon meal. Puget and his men were entirely unaware of the offense this action caused for the Indians, who held fishing rights to be sacred, and passed between generations. The visitors' failure to even ask permission before laying their nets out was a grave insult to the Indian inhabitants, who were becoming agitated.

Tensions escalated and soon the Indians and Puget's men were aiming arrows and guns at one another. But just as quickly as it started, the confrontation ended, without a shot or an arrow being fired. The two parties exchanged goods and left on friendly terms.

Over the next several days, Puget's party continued to explore the south Puget Sound, finding friendly Indians willing to present the explorers with food and goods. Puget's party took careful notes on the Indians' customs and culture, including gender roles, living conditions, and language. He returned to Vancouver's ship a week after he departed, with copious notes detailing the natural beauty of the area and the friendliness and hospitality of its people.

For the Indians Puget and his party encountered, the visit by the white men caused some tension and concern, but when they left after a short week, life went back to normal. Although Europeans and eventually, with the arrival of Meriwether Lewis and William Clark to the Pacific Ocean in 1805, Americans, explored the region, few came into direct contact with the Puyallup Tribe. In the 1820s, small groups of white traders began exploring the Puget Sound in small groups. The traders' brief visits were welcomed for the economic opportunities they provided the Tribe. Although their visits were short, they left a trail of devastation as their Indian hosts were ravaged by smallpox and other diseases against which they had no immunity. The Puyallup neighbors, the Nisqually Tribe, were especially ravaged by the white man's diseases.

Although the Puyallups did not come into direct contact with many Europeans or Americans, they heard rumors and stories about other tribes' encounters. In 1821, Hudson's Bay Company Governor George Simpson ordered the construction of Fort Vancouver near the mouth of the Willamette River. The erection of the fort encouraged settlers to stream into the Willamette Valley region, a change that had brought disease and exploitation to the Indians in that area.

Although traders brought new technology to the Indians of Puget Sound, they made no attempts to introduce religion to them. Protestant missionaries began coming into the state in the 1830s in an attempt to educate and convert the Native peoples. Oftentimes, the presence of missionaries ended with devastating consequences. The Whitman mission, established by Marcus and Narcissa Whitman in eastern Washington in 1836, was attacked by the local Cayuse Tribe, which had been devastated by the effects of measles introduced by a passing wagon train. The Whitmans and about a dozen others were killed by two Cayuse members in retaliation. In response, 500 volunteer soldiers set out to take revenge. As white traders and missionaries encroached upon Indian land and as foreign diseases ravaged Indian populations, hostilities increased. Though the Puyallup Tribe was sheltered from early influx of missionaries and traders to the state, they were not unaware of the devastation many of their neighboring tribes were facing.

The first European settlement in the Puget Sound was Fort Nisqually, which was established in 1833 by the Hudson's Bay Company, which, after the perceived success of Fort Vancouver, sought to establish similar trading posts around the Northwest.

The addition of the fort to the area brought many changes to the Puyallup Tribe and other area tribes. As Fort Nisqually quickly became a center for trade, more and more people–both Native and non-Native–came and went from the area to trade. Members of local tribes, including the Puyallups, took advantage of the trading opportunities as well as cultural opportunities. Every Sunday the fort would hold religious services that many local Indians would attend. The Hudson's Bay Company also began hiring Indians to help with farming alongside trading post residents.

Almost as soon as the fort was opened, the fur trading business began to decline. But the fort continued to thrive, as farming and animal husbandry became increasingly important activities at the fort. Members of the Puyallup Tribe regularly visited the fort not only to participate in activities, but also to trade furs and other items.

In 1839 the first missionaries arrived at the fort. Reverend David Leslie and Brother William Holden Willson arrived at the fort in April of that year and built a small mission building near the fort. In that same year a Catholic priest, Father Modesto Demers, also visited the fort. Indian people representing at least 22 tribes came to hear him speak. While many Indians were fascinated by the religious practices of the white settlers, they soon found that some of their own activities and customs—such as gambling, the use of medicine men and death and burial—were not acceptable to the white religious leaders, which paved the way for conflict.

Over the first few decades of the 1800s, settlers slowly trickled into the Northwest via what would become known as the Oregon Trail. In 1843, the first large wave of settlers—called the "great emigration"—traveled along the trail and settled in the Northwest. Though the great emigration was probably not more than 1,000 people, the event triggered a fast-growing increase in settlement in the region.

Throughout the early decades of the 1800s, the United States and Britain bickered over territory boundaries. Armed with ideas of "manifest destiny" and a slogan of "fifty-four forty or fight," Americans pushed for a territory that spread from the Atlantic to the Pacific, and from the northern boundary of what is now British Columbia south. President James Polk, who was elected in 1844, fought hard to establish such boundaries. In 1846 Polk agreed to a compromise with Britain to place the boundary along the 49th parallel, where the U.S. border with Canada is today. In 1848, the U.S. Congress established the Oregon Territory. All these decisions and agreements were carried out without the consultation of the Indians living in the area.

The first American settlement in what would become Washington state was founded in October 1845. Settler Michael T. Simmons led a wagon train from Missouri. The group settled in Tumwater, calling the location New Market. The settlement was meant to be a trading alternative to the British Fort Nisqually. At the site, Simmons built a sawmill and a gristmill and harnessed hydraulic power using Tumwater Falls.

By 1850, fewer than 500 whites were estimated to be living in the Puget Sound area. In that year, the U.S. government established two Acts that would have further devastating effects on the tribes living in the Puget Sound and the Northwest. The Oregon Donation Land Act granted each U.S. citizen 640 free acres, or one square mile, of land in the Oregon Territory. The Indian Removal Act of 1830 authorized the purchase of land from various northwest coast tribes, and permitted the removal of Indians to areas settlers did not want. This caused much tension—in two cases in southern Oregon and northern California, violence broke out. Although the Indians of Puget Sound were not involved in these events, they learned of the events and the actions that precipitated them, and their negative views toward the U.S. government and white settlers continued to grow. The growing white population—which had reached several thousand in the Puget Sound by the end of 1852—also put pressure on Puget Sound tribes.

Pioneer Ezra Meeker and his wife, Eliza Jane Sumner Meeker, arrived in the Puget Sound area in 1853. Over the following decade, the Meeker family spent time living on McNeal Island, in southeast Tacoma, and in Steilacoom before finally settling in the Puyallup valley in 1862. Although in his writings Meeker admits he initially accepted the unfair characterizations of Indians as savage and violent, his unfounded prejudice wore off. For the rest of his life, in his various writings and elsewhere, Meeker described the Indians of Puget Sound as exceptionally welcoming and giving.

One of his first meaningful encounters was when he and his brother boated through the Puget Sound in 1853. They were invited by some local Indians to join in a clambake. In Meeker's writings, this reflected a turning point in his personal relationship with the local Native Americans. "We had been in the Indian country for nearly a year, but with guns by our sides if not in our hands for nearly half the time, while on the plains, but we had not stopped to study the Indian character," he recalled decades later.

For the first part of the 19th century, the Indians of Puget Sound lived in relative harmony with the white traders and settlers who came into the region. But the situation began to change when the Washington Territory was established in 1853 and the United States began formal treaty negotiations for Indians' land. The territory's first governor, Isaac I. Stevens, a West Point graduate, former army officer and Democrat, entered Washington with the primary purpose of solidifying treaties in which Indians would cede their land to whites.

Stevens was an ardent advocate for white expansion. He hoped to remove Washington's Indians from their land and concentrate them on as few reservations as possible. Stevens saw the territory's Native populations as inferior to whites, and as impediments to advancement and expansion. He approached negotiations with tribes with these biases. Although he was a young man at 35, Stevens treated all Indians, regardless of their age, as children. He lied and manipulated Indians to get treaties signed. The new era of relations between whites and Indians—and the first official encounters between Native populations and the U.S. government—brought an end to the prevailing goodwill and brought about darker times in U.S.-Indian relations.

Portrait of Brigadier General Isaac Ingalls Stevens, first governor of Washington Territory. Stevens served as governor from 1853-1857. A Democrat, he was appointed by President Franklin Pierce. In addition, he served as Superintendent of Indian Affairs. This portrait depicts Stevens as a Brigadier General of Volunteers and may have been made ca. 1862. He was killed in action in 1862 during the Second Battle of Bull Run (Second Manassas). Copyright (c) the Board of Trustees of the Tacoma Public Library.

CHAPTER 3

MEDICINE CREEK TREATY

In the mid-1800s, Indians along the coast of the Puget Sound lived relatively undaunted by the appearance of foreigners. Members of the Puyallup Tribe, like other tribes in the area, had been in contact with workers from the British Hudson's Bay Company starting as early as 1833, and before that with Spanish explorers and other types of adventure seekers from abroad. The company's relationship with Indians from the Puyallup and Nisqually tribes was peaceful and friendly. The British saw it as good business to interact with the local Indians. The two groups had often intermarried, exchanged language and other practices, managing to create a moderately harmonious give-take, live-and-let-live relationship in the Pacific Northwest.

White settlers began to move west from the American colonies during the early part of the century, and a less than desirable stigma was created toward the Indians and vice versa. Settlers

Portrait of ancestral Puyallup Tribe leader Eel-ah-cah-cah, also known as Tyee Dick, a signer of the Medicine Creek Treaty and combatant in the treaty wars that followed. Courtesy of the Washington State Historical Society.

pushed west, forcing the Indian Territory farther and farther out until it reached the end of the line at the coast. As Americans moved west, they occupied more and more of the Indians' land, even before any formal reservation system or donation land act had been established.

They also brought with them diseases unaccustomed to the Native population, causing very poor health and even death for much of the population. The extent of damage done to the Native Americans cannot be stressed enough. A smallpox epidemic that began on the Northwest coast in the 1770s killed more than 11,000 Indians in Western Washington. It is estimated that the disease decimated at least 30 percent of the Native population on the Northwest coast and Puget Sound, while others put that figure much higher. Smallpox and other diseases, including measles and influenza, continued to ravage the people for the next 80 to 100 years and killed up to 28,000 Native Americans in Western Washington.

As settlers advanced across the nation, what was referred to as the "frontier line"—the division between Indian and white American settlers' land—could no longer exist the further settlers went, and the closer to the West Coast that they got. There was nowhere else for Indians to go save for the most undesirable land that was reserved for them when the federal government established the practice of an Indian reservation system.

In 1853 Congress separated Washington from the Oregon Territory. Isaac I. Stevens was appointed to serve as governor of Washington Territory as well as superintendent of Indian Affairs. The young man, 34 at the time, was sent to the area to assess the situation in the Northwest, and come up with suggestions for the best ways to isolate, segregate, and eventually assimilate the Indians into "civilized" white, American culture.

Studio portrait of Puyallup leader Tommy Lane (1852-1909), also known as Chief Iudyoupkin, last chief of the Puyallup Tribe. Courtesy of the Washington State Historical Society.

Negotiations between the federal government and the tribes of the region began shortly after Stevens' arrival in Washington Territory. The Treaty at Medicine Creek, the first Indian treaty in the region, would establish a precedent that included misleading Indians and taking control of vast areas of their land to be repeated with several other tribes and Indian regions in the state. It would prompt unrest and war among Indians and whites on both sides of the Cascades, establishing a long-standing skepticism among Indians toward the American government.

The treaty would also establish a framework for the future of Indian rights and sovereignty which the Puyallup Tribe stands by today. The government's practices and intentions at the time were scrutinized by both Indians and non-Indians as the treaty had more or less established a precedent for unethical mistreatment of the Puyallups and other tribes that lasted well into the 20th century. At the same time the treaty allowed the Puyallup Tribe to establish in the document their sovereignty and rights assigned to them, which has played a key role in the success of the tribes today, even though they were not fully realized until much later.

In 1854 Stevens was charged with removing Indians' titles to their land in the Washington Territory in order to free more land for settlers who were coming to the area, keeping the two populations as segregated as possible. The idea was to appeal to the settlers because they would not have to interact with or fear the Indians, and to appeal to the Indians because they would have their own land to carry on their accustomed practices.

However, the amount of land and location of the reservations that were initially designated to the Puyallup, Nisqually, and Squaxin Island tribes were far from what they were accustomed to. They were granted about 1,200 acres each for their entire populations (Squaxin received less because of the predetermined size of Squaxin Island). The Oregon Donation Land Act of 1850 supplied 320 acres to single men settling in the Northwest, and 640 acres to families or married men. At the time, the Washington area, along with the Coast Salish tribes, fell within the Oregon Territory. Settlers had already been taking up cleared lands from the Indian people, but now the government had made it official, and encouraged it. Settlers began to pour into the area at the offer of hundreds of free acres of land for their families to settle on. Indians were further displaced from their homes.

After the conclusion of the Medicine Creek Treaty Council, which included reservations for the Puyallup, Nisqually, and Squaxin Island tribes, Stevens had acquired 2.5 million acres, which previously belonged to the Indians. The Indians, totaling well more than 1,000 at the time, were granted 3,840 acres for their use. The acreage granted to the three tribes of Indians after the Treaty of Medicine Creek in 1854 would have equaled the amount of land granted to 12 families through the Donation Land Act. The reservation lands were also poorly situated in areas that were not suitable for the tribes' accustomed practices such as fishing, hunting, and gathering. Land that was undesirable to the settlers and the government was designated as home to hundreds of Indians. Indians who identified with smaller tribes and bands other than the three reservation tribes were forced to pick a reservation to associate with.

At the time, Stevens assumed that all Coast Salish Indian people were the same, when in actuality the array of tribes and bands in the region were often very culturally diverse. On Christmas Eve, the Indians were told a potlatch was being held at the site of the treaty negotiations at the mouth of Medicine

Puyallup couple Burnt Face Charley and his wife, taken ca. 1900. Courtesy of the Washington State Historical Society.

Creek near the Nisqually River. Using the potlatch as a ruse, Indian agents for the U.S. government were able to identify delegates and leaders for each tribe to represent their people in the negotiations process. The delegates were promised a potlatch, and that the treaty would provide justice for all involved. What the Indians received at the conclusion of the treaty negotiations was a document that relinquished almost all of the Indian title to the government, a misinterpreted explanation of the terms of the treaty, and promises for goods and services—not money—all of which was never fully realized by the tribal parties involved. In addition, the treaty was interpreted in Chinook jargon rather than the tribes' native language, making it difficult if not impossible for tribal leaders to know exactly what they were being asked to sign.

Stevens, along with Indian Agent Michael Simmons, Secretary to the Commission James Doty, interpreter Benjamin Shaw, George Gibbs, secretary for Washington Territory, C.H. Mason and Lieutenant William Slaughter met with about 700 Indians from the affected tribes and bands for negotiations that would last two days. Several other white witnesses were also present during the negotiations. Stevens read a speech to the group, expressing the terms of the treaty he wished the Indians to sign. They would hand over the majority of their land in exchange for concentrated areas that would be for their "exclusive use," and also receive goods and services such as doctors, schoolteachers, and a blacksmith, from the federal government.

"The great father...wishes you to have homes, pasture for your horses, and fishing places. He wishes you to learn to farm and your children to go to a good school. And now he wants me to make a bargain with you, in which you will sell your lands and in return be provided with all these things."—Isaac Stevens,

1854

Stevens' words were translated by Shaw and Simmons in Chinook jargon, a language that was common in trading practices throughout Indian country, but not understood by most of the Puget Sound people.

Later testimony from Indians who were present at the time of the negotiations revealed that they did not fully understand the terms they agreed to. Many believed they were getting a better deal than they received, otherwise they would have never agreed to the treaty terms.

"Did you understand what the treaty was?"
"No, I don't think any of the Indians understand. Why would they agree to give up all the good land, and that was what we found afterwards the treaty read."
—Testimony of influential Puyallup tribal member Tyee Dick to settler Ezra Meeker in 1904

Influential Indian leader Chief Leschi of the Nisqually Tribe and his brother Queimuth were not satisfied with the terms of the treaty when they were read at Medicine Creek. Some documents and oral histories relate that Leschi and Queimuth did not sign the treaty and left with about 50 men at the end of the first night of negotiations. However, an "X" was marked next to each of the brothers' names on the formal treaty document, along with an "X" beside the names of 60 other Indians. Debate remains to this day over whether or not these men actually made the simple "X" themselves or if the mark was forged.

Nevertheless, the treaty was "signed" the evening of the second day of negotiations, Dec. 26, 1854, and with 19 American men as witness. The final document was ratified by Congress

Treaty trees at Medicine Creek (now on the property of A.L. Brown Farm), where the Medicine Creek Treaty was negotiated and signed. Photograph by Asahel Curtis. Courtesy of the Washington State Historical Society.

Mount Tacoma, now known as Mount Rainier. Courtesy of the Tacoma Public Library.

Puyallup tribal members known as Adam and Eve (writing on photo states that their age is unknown). Courtesy of the Washington State Capital Museum Collection.

on March 3, 1855 and includes 13 articles outlining the treaty parameters, Indian rights, restrictions, and sovereignty.

Highlights from the Treaty are as follows:

- Reservations were to be "marked out for their exclusive use," "nor shall any white man be permitted to reside upon the same without permission of the tribe or superintendent or agent." All Indians "agree to remove to and settle upon the same within one year after the ratification of this treaty."

- The treaty spelled out the Indians' "right of taking fish at all usual and accustomed grounds and stations…together with the privilege of hunting, gathering roots and berries, and pasturing their horses."

- "The United States agree to pay…the sum of $32,500 (over 20 years, with annual sums decreasing every few years); all which said sums of money shall be applied to the use and benefit of the said Indians, under the direction of the President of the United States, who may from time to time determine, at his discretion, upon what beneficial objects to expend the same. And the superintendent of Indian affairs…shall each year inform the President of the wishes of said Indians…."

- "The president may hereafter, when in his opinion the interest of the Territory may require, and the welfare of the said Indians be promoted, remove them from either or all of said reservations to such other suitable place or places within said Territory as he may deem fit…"

- "He may further…cause…the land as may be selected in lieu thereof, to be surveyed into lots, and assign the same to such individual or families…"

- The United States agreed to establish "an agricultural and industrial school, to be free to the children of the said tribes and bands, in common with those of the other tribes of said district, and to provide the said school with a suitable instructor or instructors, and also to provide a smithy and carpenter's shop, and carpenter, and farmer, for the term of 20 years, to instruct the Indians in their respective occupations."

- The government also promised to "furnish medicine and advice to their sick and shall vaccinate them; the expenses of the said school, shops, employees and medical attendance, to be defrayed by the United States and not deducted from the annuities."

Sixty-two delegates of the Nisqually, Puyallup, Steilacoom, Squaxin, S'Homamish, Stehchass, T'Peeksin, Squi'aitl, and Sa-heh-wamish tribes and bands were present at the treaty signing. For the purpose of the treaty, all tribes and bands were regarded as one nation despite their differing customs and cultures, and the fact that they represented only a fraction of the Indians in the Puget Sound region.

During negotiations, more land was requested to be included in the reservations, but Stevens argued it was unnecessary because of the favorable location of the lands. The approximately 1,200 acres for the Puyallup reservation was originally located in what is now downtown Tacoma. The rectangular block, one by two miles in area, was stationed on the bluff overlooking Commencement Bay, approximately where the historic Stadium High School sits currently. Several small Puyallup villages were already located in that general area, but they were far removed from the people's beloved river that had given so many blessings to the Tribe for countless generations. It offered them not only food the people needed to live well; the river was then (and continues to be today) a source of spiritual sustenance. Like a mother provides for her children, the people's connection to the river ran just as deep. Being away from the river was a

Tommy Lane's residence on the Puyallup Reservation. Courtesy of the Washington State Historical Society.

The Taylor family home, on the Puyallup Reservation. Courtesy of the Washington State Historical Society.

Pow wow of Puyallup Indians. A large group of men and three dogs stand outside a large wooden house on the Puyallup Indian Reservation on Feb. 9, 1891. Several women and children are visible in the background, standing in the doorway of the house. Thomas H. Rutter, photographer. Courtesy of the Washington State Historical Society.

In this circa 1886 photograph, a Native American family lounges in their canoe near the shore. In the background can be seen the Northern Pacific Railroad bridge. The canoe is loaded with supplies, probably returning or setting off for the family's hunting ground. The Puyallup Tribe members were primarily hunters, gatherers and fishermen. During this time period their village was believed to be located at the foot of South 15th Street. Courtesy of the Tacoma Public Library.

cruel thing to do to the people, as they longed to be on the banks of the flowing waters.

Stevens' plan was to put more than 500 Puyallups on 1,200 acres, which equated to about the same acreage two families of settlers would have received under the Donation Land Act established four years prior.

Following the ratification of the treaty, Tribal members began to feel taken advantage of. The reservations were too small and the land that was surveyed for the reservations did not match the land that was agreed to in the treaty. Hostilities began to arise among Indians east of the Cascades because of conflicts with the settlers and government practices there. Hostilities arose west of the Cascades because of influence from the Eastern Washington Indians and because of aggravation with the Americans based on the treaty. War eventually broke out as Indians rebelled against the unfair stipulations of the treaties they had been misled to agree to over the last year.

In letters to Stevens at the end of 1856, Special Indian Agent for the United States Government Wesley B. Gosnell described the Indian/white conflict. He stated that the "principle portion of the hostilities west of the Cascades…were from the Puyallup and Nisqually tribes." Indians east of the Cascades had been reported to have threatened coastal Indians if they did not support their feelings of hostility towards Americans. "The upper Nisquallies, upper Puyallups, a portion of the Lower Puyallups, the Clickitats, and other Indians living near the head of the Green and White Rivers…at once entered into the combination. The other Indians of the Sound, their sympathies with the hostiles, but afraid of the whites on the one hand, and equally in terror of the execution of the threats of the Indians east of the mountains on the other, hesitated, and stood for some time in a balance as it were for peace or for war. Meanwhile those who were in favor of the plan used every effort to make the combination adapted to work upon the fears and cruelty of an ignorant and uncivilized people…"

Gosnell insisted that the reasons for war were only to "a limited degree at the hands of the whites." He described what he felt were, in his opinion, the "real" causes of why Indians west of the Cascades took up arms against whites as follows:

• Yakamas, Klickitats, and Walla Wallas threatened to kill or make slaves of anyone who failed to make common cause with them.

• Encouragement from foreigners in the Territory (the British reportedly supplied Puget Sound Indians with ammunition).

• Indians were afraid of being wiped out by whites, and saw it as good timing to exterminate them.

Shortly after the signing of the Medicine Creek Treaty, Leschi peacefully met with government officials on several occasions to try to get better reservations for the tribes. When he was told it was "too late" he knew war was inevitable. Warring carried on between the Puget Sound Indians and whites from the fall of 1855 to the spring of 1856. Volunteer militias ordered by Acting Governor Charles Mason fought the warring Indians, while "friendly" Indians were forced into a yearlong internment at Fox Island. This completely uprooted the lives of the families that were held there. They were guarded and watched day and night, and fed meals sent by the territorial government. Like the U.S. Japanese internment camps of World War II, being held at Fox Island was like being a prisoner in a military encampment.

Stevens believed the militias were essential to protecting the settlers from the hostile Indians. He also believed intern-

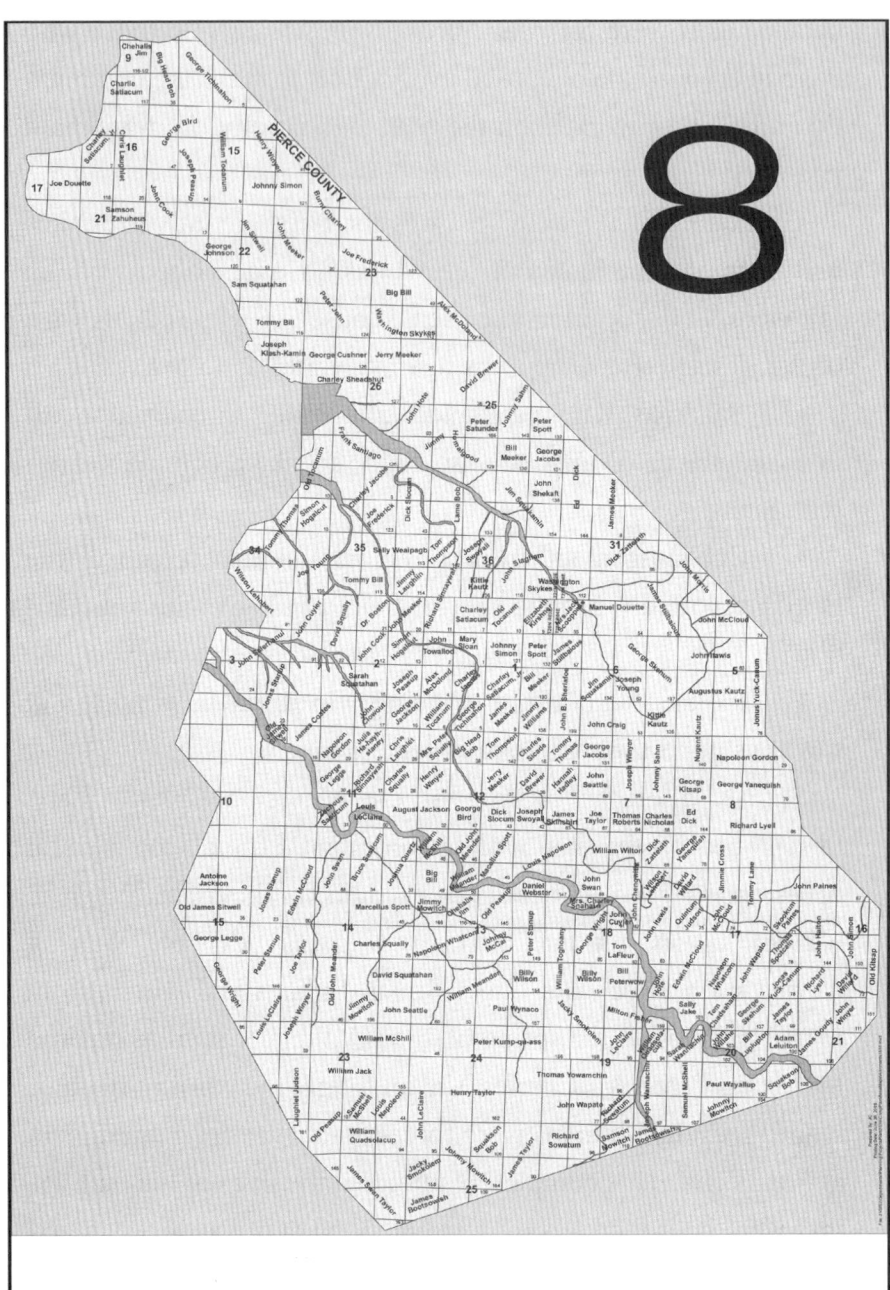

ALLOTMENTS 1886

ing other Indians was in order to keep them from joining their hostile peers. Blockhouses were built along the Puget Sound for protection of settlers. Many families retreated to these blockhouses, while several old-time settlers, such as Ezra Meeker, and whites who had established family ties with the Indians, did not fear the warriors.

After the war in Puget Sound began to die down, Stevens called another council in August 1856. The two-day Fox Island Peace Council was held with the "friendly Indians" who had been interned at Fox Island. It was Stevens' intention to renegotiate the reservation boundaries in hopes to appease the hostile Indians after disapproval from government officials, most notably Col. John Wool, who regularly disagreed with Stevens' handling of the Indian Wars. During the Fox Island council, Governor Stevens did his best to convince the councilmen that he and the federal government were only looking out for their best interest. In Cecilia Svinth Carpenter's book "Tears of Internment: The Indian History of Fox Island and the Puget Sound Indian War," the author presents a transcription of one of Stevens' speeches to the Indian Council at Fox Island, 1856. He referred to the council as "children" and "my children" repeatedly, and attempted to convince the Council that there would be no trickery involved in negotiations to expand the reservation. "I am sure I will try not to lie," he said.

Stevens accused the internees of making bad choices in the location of the reservations, even though the Indians had little to no say in it. Neither reservation Gibbs surveyed matched the locations marked on the map at the Medicine Creek Treaty negotiations.

"I am sorry that we have trouble and that we have had war. I am glad that the war is now over. We made a treaty at established reservations at the Nisqually and the Puyaloop. Those (reservations) were suggested by yourselves. I had those reserves surveyed. I found them not good."—Stevens, 1856

Nevertheless, reservation boundaries outlined at Medicine Creek were renegotiated, making them larger and in more suitable locations, such as on the Nisqually and Puyallup rivers, which the Indians had been dependent on for countless generations. Stevens also granted land between the White and Green rivers to the Upper Puyallups.

The following is an excerpt of Stevens' speech from recorded minutes of the 1856 Fox Island Council (certified record of the National Archives of the United States):

"Now my children, when we made that treaty, it was you that wanted the Res. specified. I had the two grounds examined and told Col. Simmons they were not fit for you. And last April I sent Col. Shaw to tell Leschi that the Res. were not good and Leschi sent word that my word was good. Now I do not speak of this to punish poor Leschi. You yourselves one half a year ago selected these two Res. We had them surveyed and found them unsuitable for you. We sent you word accordingly. Half of you go to war saying you are not satisfied! What can I know of your minds today! You talked today of four Res., one on the Nisqually, one at the Ste le coom Creek, one at the Potato Ground and one at the Puyaloop. How do I know by past experience what course you will pursue in the future? Have you thought it well over? Now I will agree to two Res. and no more. Those Res. shall be larger than the first selected. You shall have a large Res. at Nisqually, one large Res. on the Puyaloop. The Indians have in their treaty a right to pasturage anywhere in the territory. I say this not to you because one half has been war ground, but because it is so stated in the Treaty. I stand by that truly which says if these Res. prove insufficient they shall be enlarged. Now my children do you want a Res. on the Nisqually and one on the Puyaloop? I will send word to the Great Father if you want Res. at those places.

"Those Res. shall give you ground enough for horses and to the Horse Indians I will give land between White and Green rivers and I will send a man with you to mark out the ground so that you may be satisfied. I now wish to know if this is the word I shall send to your Great Father. I now want all of you to tell me your desires. Speak freely and truthfully."

About 700 Indians stemming from various tribes remained interned on Fox Island from the beginning of the war until January 1857, an extra four months after the war had ended and the reservations had been expanded. The Puyallup Reservation was formally surveyed in 1874.

Gosnell, a government agent charged with overseeing the Puyallup and Nisqually tribes through the era of the Indian Wars and after the Fox Island council, visited each of the reservations throughout November 1856 to see how the tribes were faring. Construction of 12 Indian houses was in the planning stages, and only 200 Indians were on the Puyallup Reservation at the time.

"They are in very destitute condition both as regards clothing and food. They are also very unhealthy and are dying off rapidly. Catholic priests have probably more influence with them than any other tribe on the Sound."

The Puyallup Tribe received more than 18,061.5 acres with farmland at the southeast end of Commencement Bay at the end of negotiations at Fox Island. The "horse Indians," the Upper Puyallups that owned and bred horses, received 3,500 acres that later became the Muckleshoot Reservation. Nisqually received 4,717 acres and Squaxin Island's reservation remained unchanged.

Records show that the Puyallup reservation boundaries extended by thousands of acres from what was finally decided upon by both parties in 1873, by Executive Order, and the final decision of creating the allotment map in 1886. The largest numbers of Indian families were forced to go to the reservation at Puyallup. The allotments in 1886 assigned specific areas to these families. In total there were 168 allotments made at Puyallup. One small area, later named Indian Addition, was the only property held in common ownership by the Tribe.

Congress awarded a land grant to the Northern Pacific Railroad to build a line from Lake Superior to Puget Sound. In 1873 the railroad announced that it would build its terminus on Commencement Bay. It would name its city "Tacoma," after the Puyallups' mountain Tacobet. Consistent reports back to the eastern part of the country about the valuable land and waterfront marred any possibility of the Puyallups living contentedly upon a reserve.

Congress appointed several commissions to study the reservation and the potential sale of lands thereon. Taxation leases and misunderstanding of property law resulted in almost the entire reservation going out of Tribal ownership early on. There were guardians appointed to the Puyallups (if they resisted selling their lands); some leaders were even mysteriously murdered. An uncanny number of Puyallup allottees were found dead on railroad tracks, casting doubt on how exactly they had died, as some believe desire for the victim's allotment property could have been a motive for murder. Authorities blamed their deaths on alcoholism, being struck by railroad trains, and often both "causes" were cited. By eight years after the allotments were made, one-third of the original allottees were dead.

A study of reports from the early 1900s by sources such as the Pierce County Coroner's Office, U.S. Department of Interior, and local newspapers concerning area Indian deaths reveal a disturbing pattern:

• John Salerhanul—"…struck by a railroad train…," Dept. of Interior, 1888

• Tommy Thomas—"…he had been drinking…was found lying at the foot of the embankment near the track, dead," Dept. of Interior, 1900

• Albert J. Kautz—"…struck by railway train…," Washington State Burial Permit, 1914

• James Bill—"…struck by an Interurban Tacoma-bound train…was so intoxicated he could hardly walk…," Tacoma Ledger, 1905

The pattern continues: Dick Zadtlath and wife Sarah Grenon–both killed by railway train; Jimmy Coats—fell off train trestle and died; Lollie Napoleon—run over by switch engine, legs severed. This is just a small sampling of the many incidents of such deaths that appear suspicious.

In her book "The Puyallup-Nisqually," Marian Smith writes: "When the whites introduced the concept of accidental death, it was quickly adopted as an alternative to murder. A man plotting another man's death pretended friendship, invited his intended victim to a drinking bout in which he himself only apparently participated and, when the other was drunk, killed him and placed the body on the railroad track where the next train could be relied upon to eradicate all evidence of personal violence. There is no doubt that a majority of the accidents recorded as man-drunk-falls-asleep-on-tracks-on-way-home actually came within such a category. Deeds of this type, which fell outside the concept of murder as it had once existed, did not, according to my informants, require any purification. It was almost impossible to apprehend murderers in white courts for these convincing 'accident' victims. Informants went so far as to say that the rapid decrease in the numbers of Indians on the Puyallup reservation between 1895 and 1900 was as much due to this form of murder as to disease. Of course, alcohol served to spur on the murderer in many cases."

By 1950 there were approximately ten families who still owned their assigned lands in whole or in part. A stubborn persistence of even the Bureau of Indian Affairs (BIA) in not recognizing the reservation prevailed. Thirty acres and several parcels that were being leased remained.

5

Dec. 24th   Governor Stevens left Olympia and proceeded
to the Treaty Ground on the She-nah-nam or Medicine
Creek.

Dec. 25th   The Programme of the Treaty was fully
explained to the Indians present.

At the evening session of the Commission the draft of
the proposed Treaty was read, and after a full discussion
of its provisions by the gentlemen present, viz. Messrs.
Simmons, Shaw and Doty, it was directed to be engrossed
and is as follows:

Articles of agreement and convention, made and concluded
on the She-nah-nam or Medicine Creek, in the Territory of
Washington, this twenty sixth day of December, in the year One
thousand Eight hundred and fifty-four, by Isaac I. Stevens
Governor & Superintendent of Indian Affairs of the said Territory
on the part of the United States, and the undersigned Chiefs, Head
men, and Delegates of the Nisqually, Puyallup, Steilacoom,
Squawksin, S'Homamish, Stehchass, T'Peeksin, Squai-
aitl and Sah-heh-wamish Tribes and Bands of Indians,
occupying the lands lying around the head of Puget's Sound
and the adjacent Inlets, who for the purpose of this Treaty are to
be regarded as one Nation, on behalf of said Tribes and Bands
and duly authorized by them:

Art. 1   The said Tribes and Bands of Indians hereby cede,
relinquish and convey to the United States all their right,
title and interest in and to the lands and country occupied
by them, bounded and described as follows, to wit:

Commencing at the point on the Eastern side of
Admiralty Inlet, known as Point Pully, about midway between Commencement and Elliotts' Bays; thence running
in a South Easterly direction, following the divide between
the waters of the Puyallup & Dwamish or White Rivers
to the summit of the Cascade Mountains, thence southerly
along the summit of said Range to a point opposite the
main source of the Skookum Chuck Creek, thence to and
down said Creek to the Coal Mine, thence Northwesterly
to the summit of the Black Hills, thence Northwesterly
to the upper forks of the Sat-sop River, thence Northwesterly
through the passage known as Wilkes' Portage to
Point Southworth on the Western side of Admiralty
Inlet, thence around the foot of Vashon Island Easterly and
South Easterly to the place of beginning.

Art. II   There is however reserved for the present use and occupation of the said Tribes and Bands, the following tracts of land viz:

The small island called Klah-che-min, situated opposite the mouth of Hammersley's and Totten's Inlets, and separated from Hartstene Island by Peale's passage, containing about two sections of land by estimation. A square tract containing two sections or twelve hundred and eighty acres, on Puget's Sound near the mouth of the She-nah-nam Creek, one mile west of the meridian line of the United States land survey, and a square tract containing two sections or twelve hundred and eighty acres lying on the south side of Commencement Bay, all which tracts shall be set apart, and so far as necessary surveyed and marked out for their exclusive use. Nor shall any white man be permitted to reside upon the same without permission of the Tribe and the Superintendent and Agent. And the said tribes and bands agree to remove to and settle upon the same within one year after the ratification of this treaty, or sooner if the means are furnished them. In the meantime it shall be lawful for them to reside upon any ground not in the actual claim and occupation of citizens of the United States, and upon any ground claimed or occupied if with the permission of the owner or claimant. If necessary for the public convenience, roads may be run through their reserves, and on the other hand the right of way with free access from the same to the nearest public highway is secured to them.

Art. III.   The right of taking fish at all usual and accustomed grounds and stations, is further secured to said Indians, in common with all citizens of the Territory, and of erecting temporary houses for the purpose of curing, together with the privilege of hunting, gathering roots and berries and pasturing their horses upon open and unclaimed lands. Provided however that they shall not take shell fish from any beds staked or cultivated by citizens, and that they shall alter all stallions not intended for breeding horses and shall keep up and confine the latter.

Art. IV.   In consideration of the above cession, the United States agree to pay to the said Tribes and Bands the sum of Thirty two thousand five hundred dollars in the following manner, that is to say. For the first year after the ratification hereof, three thousand two hundred and fifty dollars; for the next two years, three thousand dollars each year; for the next three years, two thousand dollars each year; for the next four years, fifteen hundred dollars each year; for the next five years, twelve hundred dollars each year; and for the next five years, One thousand dollars each year; all which said sums of money shall be applied to the use and benefit of the said Indians under the direction of the President of the United States, who may from time to time determine at his discretion upon what beneficial objects to expend the same. And the Superintendent of Indian Affairs, or other proper officer, shall each year inform the President of the wishes of the Indians in respect thereto.

Art. V.   To enable the said Indians to remove to and settle upon their aforesaid reservations, and to clear, fence and break up a sufficient quantity of land for cultivation, the United States further agree to pay the sum of three thousand two hundred and fifty dollars, to be laid out and expended under the direction of the President and in such manner as he shall approve.

Art. VI.   The President may hereafter, when in his opinion the interests of the Territory may require, and the welfare of the said Indians be promoted, remove them from either or all of said reservations to such other suitable place or places within said Territory as he may deem fit, on remunerating them for their improvements and the expenses of their removal, or may consolidate them with other friendly tribes or bands. And he may further, at his discretion, cause the whole or any portion of the lands hereby reserved, or of such other land as may be selected in lieu thereof, to be surveyed into lots, and assign the same to such individuals or families as are willing to avail themselves of the privilege, and will locate on the same as a permanent home, on the same terms and subject to the same regulations as are provided in the sixth article of the treaty with the Omahas, so far as the same may be applicable. Any substantial improvements heretofore made by any Indian, and which he shall be compelled to abandon in consequence of this treaty, shall be valued under the direction of the President, and payment be made accordingly therefor.

Art. VII.   The annuities of the aforesaid tribes and bands shall not be taken to pay the debts of individuals.

Art. VIII.   The aforesaid tribes and bands acknowledge their dependence on the government of the United States, and promise to be friendly with all citizens thereof, and pledge themselves to commit no depredations on the property of such citizens. And should any one or more of them violate this pledge, and the fact be satisfactorily proved before the Agent, the property taken shall be returned, or in default thereof, or if injured or destroyed, compensation may be made by the Government out of the annuities. Nor will they make war on any other tribe except in self defence, but will submit all matters of difference between them and other Indians to the Government of the United States or its Agent for decision and abide thereby. And if any of the said Indians commit any depredations on any other Indians within the Territory, the same rule shall prevail as that prescribed in this article in cases of depredations against Citizens. And the said tribes agree not to shelter or conceal offenders against the laws of the United States, but to deliver them up to the authorities for trial.

Art. IX. The above tribes and bands are desirous to exclude from their reservations the use of ardent spirits, and to prevent their people from drinking the same, and therefore it is provided that any Indian belonging to said tribes, who is guilty of bringing liquor into said reservation, or who drinks liquor, may have his or her proportion of the annuities withheld from him or her, for such time as the President may determine.

Art. X. The United States further agree to establish, at the general Agency for the District of Puget's Sound, within one year from the ratification hereof, and to support for a period of twenty years, an agricultural and industrial school, to be free to the children of said tribes and bands in common with those of the other tribes of said District, and to provide the said school with a suitable instructor or instructors, and also to provide a smithy and carpenters shop, and furnish them with the necessary tools, and employ a blacksmith, carpenter and farmer for the term of twenty years to instruct the Indians in their respective occupations. And the United States further agree to employ a Physician, to reside at the said Central Agency, who shall furnish medicine and advice to their sick, and shall vaccinate them; the expenses of the said school, shops, employees and medical attendance, to be defrayed by the United States and not deducted from the annuities.

Art. XI. The said tribes and bands agree to free all slaves now held by them, and not to purchase or acquire others hereafter.

Art. XII. The said tribes and bands finally agree not to trade at Vancouver's Island, or elsewhere out of the dominions of the United States; nor shall foreign Indians be permitted to reside in their reservations without consent of the Superintendent or Agent

Art. XIII. This Treaty shall be obligatory on the contracting parties as soon as the same shall be ratified by the President and Senate of the United States.

In testimony whereof the said Isaac I. Stevens, Governor and Superintendent of Indian Affairs, and the undersigned Chiefs, Head men, and Delegates of the aforesaid Tribes and Bands, have hereunto set their hands and Seals, at the place, and in the day and year hereinbefore written.

Executed in the presence of us (Signed.)
(Signed.)

M. T. Simmons, Indian Agent
James Doty, Secy of the Commission
C. N. Mason, Capt. Wash. Terry.
W. A. Slaughter, 1st Lieut. 4th Infty
James McAlister
E. Giddings Jr.
George Shazer
Henry D. Cock
S. S. Ford Jr.
Jno. W. McAlister
Cromwell Cushman
Peter Anderson
Samuel Klady
W. H. Pullen
P. O. Hough
E. R. Tyrell
George Gibbs
Benj. F. Shaw, Interpreter
Hazard Stevens

Isaac I. Stevens [L.S.]
Gov. & Supt Ter. Wash.

Qui-ee-metl × [L.S.]
Sno-ho-dum-set × [L.S.]
Seah-high × [L.S.]
Slip-o-elm × [L.S.]
Kwi-ats × [L.S.]
Stee-high × [L.S.]
Dina-kih × [L.S.]
Hi-ten × [L.S.]
Squa-ha-hud × [L.S.]
Kahk-tee-mish × [L.S.]
Smew-a-quitt × [L.S.]
Al-tah × [L.S.]
Sahl-ko-min × [L.S.]
Tlat-stu-hih-bit × [L.S.]
Tcha-hows-tan × [L.S.]
Hu-cha-not × [L.S.]
Shem-pah × [L.S.]

Swe-yah-tum	X	SS
Chah-achah	X	SS
Pih-kiho	X	SS
S'klah-o-sum	X	SS
Sah-ke-lath	X	SS
See-lup	X	SS
E-lah-bah-ka	X	SS
Slug-yah	X	SS
Wi-nuk	X	SS
Ma-mo-nich	X	SS
Chielo	X	SS
Snutoamo	X	SS
Bets-le-kobo	X	SS
Hin-e-yo	X	SS
Klo-out	X	SS
Se-uch-ka-naw	X	SS
Ska-mah-haw	X	SS
Wute-um-a-pund	X	SS
Quats-a-laaw	X	SS
Quats-a-heh-mtow	X	SS
Yah-uh-chw	X	SS
To-lahl-kut	X	SS
Yul-lout	X	SS

See-ahts-oot-soot.	X	S.S.
Ye-lah-ko.	Y	S.S.
Wee-pe-it-ew.	X	S.S.
Nah-ste.	X	S.S.
Kah-hem-kaw.	X	S.S.
Puh-how-at-iah.	V	S.S.
Swe-yehow.	X	S.S.
Sah-h-ill.	V	S.S.
Se-hwaht.	X	S.S.
Nah-hum-tilts	X	S.S.
Yah-kwe-bah.	X	S.S.
Hut-sah-le-nuw.	X	S.S.
Sah-ba-hat.	X	S.S.
Til-a-kiah.	X	S.S.
Swe-keh-naw.	X	S.S.
Sit-oo-ah.	X	S.S.
Ko-gul-a-cut.	X	S.S.
Jack.	X	S.S.
Kah-kiw-h-le.	X	S.S.
Go-yeh-hw.	X	S.S.
Sah-putch.	X	S.S.
William.	X	S.S.

TREATY OF MEDICINE CREEK - 1854

Between the United States and the Nisqually, Puyallup, Steilacoom, Squaxin, Samamish, Stechass, T'Peeksin, Squiatl, and Sahehwamish tribes.

Article 1. The said tribes and bands of Indians hereby cede, relinquish, and convey to the United States, all their right, title, and interest in and to Wit: Commencing at the on the eastern side of Admiralty Inlet known as Point Pully, about midway between commencement and Elliott Bays; thence southerly, along the summit of said range, to a point opposite the main source of the Skookum Chuck Creek; thence to and down said creek, to the coal mine; thence northwesterly, to the summit of the Black Hills thence northerly, to the upper forks of the Satsop River; thence north-easterly, through the portage known as Wilkes's Portage, to the Point Southworth, on the western side of Admiralty Inlet; thence around the foot of Vashon's Island, easterly and southeasterly, to the place of beginning.

Article 2. There is, however, reserved for the present use and occupation of the said tribes and bands, the following tracts of land, viz: The small Island called Klah-che-min, situated opposite the mouths of Hammersley's and Totten Inlets and separated from Hartstene Island by Peale's Passage, containing about two sections of land by estimation; a square tract containing two sections, or twelve hundred and eight acres, on Puget's Sound, near the mouth of She-nah-nam Creek, one mile west of the meridian line of the United States land survey, and a square tract containing two sections or twelve hundred and fifty acres, lying on the south side of Commencement Bay; all which tracts shall be set apart, and, so far as necessary, surveyed and marked out for their exclusive use; nor shall any white man be permitted to reside upon the same without permission of the Tribe and the superintendent or agent. And the said tribes and bands agree to remove to and settle upon the same within one year after the ratification of this treaty, or sooner if the means are furnished them. In the mean time, it shall be lawful for them to reside upon any ground not in the actual claim and occupation of citizens of the United States, and upon any ground claimed or occupied, if with the permission of the owner of Claimant. If necessary for the public convenience, roads may be run through their reserves, and, on the other hand, the right of way with free access from the same to the nearest public highway is secured to them.

Article 3. The right of taking fish, at all usual accustomed grounds and stations, is further secured to said Indians in common with all citizens of the Territory, and of erecting temporary houses for the purpose of curing, together with the privilege of hunting, gathering roots and berries, and pasturing their horses on open and unclaimed lands: Provided, however, that they shall not take shellfish from and beds staked or cultivated by citizens, and that they shall after all stallions not intended for breeding-horses, and shall keep up and confine the latter.

Article 4. In consideration of the above session, the United States agree to pay to the said tribes and bands the sum of thirty-two thousand five hundred dollars, in the following manner that is to say: For the first year after the ratification hereof, three thousand two hundred and fifty dollars; for the next two years, three thousand dollars each year; for the next three years, two thousand dollars each year; and for the next five years, one-thousand dollars; all which said sums of money shall be applied to the use and benefit of the said Indians under the direction of the President of the United States, who may from time determine, at his discretion, upon what beneficial objects to expend the same. And the superintendent of Indian affairs, or other proper officer, shall each year inform the President of the wishes of said Indians in respect thereto.

Article 5. To enable the said Indians to remove to and settle upon their aforesaid reservations, and to clear, fence, and break up a sufficient quantity of land for cultivation, the United States further agree to pay expended under the direction of the President, and in such manner as he shall approve.

Article 6. The President may hereafter, when in his opinion the interests of the Territory may require, and the welfare of the said Indians be promoted, remove them from some or all of said reservations to such other suitable place or places within said Territory as he may deem fit, on renumbering them for their improvements and the expenses of their removal, or may consolidate them with other land as may be selected on lieu thereof, to be surveyed into lots, and assign the same to such individuals or families as are willing to avail themselves of the privilege, and will locate on the same as are provided in the sixth article of the treaty with the Omahas, so far as the same may be applicable. Any substantial improvements heretofore made by any Indian, and which he shall be compelled to abandon in consequence of this treaty, shall be valued under the direction of the President, and payment be made accordingly therefore.

Article 7. The annuities of the aforesaid tribes and bands shall not be taken to pay the debts of individuals.

Article 8. The aforesaid tribes and bands acknowledge their dependence on the Government of the United States, and promise to be friendly with all citizens thereof, and pledge themselves to commit no depredations on the property of such citizens. And should any one or more of them violate this pledge, and the fact be satisfactorily proved before the agent, the property taken shall be returned, or in default thereof, or if injured or destroyed, compensation may be made by the Government out of their annuities. Nor will they make war on any other tribe except in self-defense, but will submit all matters of difference between them and other Indians to the Government of the United States, or its agent, for decision, and abide thereby. And if any of the said Indians commit any depredations on any other Indians within the Territory, the same rule shall prevail as that prescribed in this article, in cases of depredations against citizens. And the said tribes agree not to shelter or conceal offenders against the laws of the United States, but to deliver them up to the authorities for a trial.

Article 9. The above tribes and bands are desirous to exclude from their reservations the use of ardent spirits, and to prevent their people from drinking the same, and therefore it is provided, that any Indian belonging to said tribes, who is guilty of bringing liquor into said Reservations, or who drink liquor, may have his or her proportion of the annuities with-held from him or her for such time as the President may determine

Article 10. The United States further agree to establish at the general agency for the district of Puget's Sound, within one year from the ratification hereof, and to support, for a period of twenty years, an agricultural and industrial school, to be free to children of the said tribes and bands, in common with those of the other tribes of said district, and to provide the said school with a suitable instruction or instructors, and also to provide a smithy and carpenter's shop, and furnish them with the necessary tools, and employ a blacksmith, carpenter, and farmer for the term of twenty years, to instruct the Indians in their respective occupations. And the United States further agree to employ a physician to reside at the said central agency who shall furnish medicine and advice to their sick, and shall vaccinate them; the expenses of the said school, shops, employees, and medical attendance, to be defrayed by the United States, and not deducted from the annuities.

Article 11. The said tribes and bands agree to free all slaves now held by them, and not to purchase or acquire others hereafter.

Article 12. The said tribes and bands finally agree not to trade at Vancouver's Island, or elsewhere out to the dominions of the United States; nor shall foreign Indians be permitted to reside in their reservations without consent of the superintendent or agent.

Article 13. This treaty shall be obligatory on the contracting parties as soon as the same shall be ratified by the President and Senate of the United States.

CHAPTER 4

EDUCATION AND HEALTH OF FAMILIES AND CHILDREN

A condition of the Medicine Creek Treaty, signed by the Puyallups in 1854, was the construction of an Indian school, which would be provided to children of the Medicine Creek Treaty tribes free for 20 years following. The school would be funded and run by the federal government. The first school established was on Squaxin Island, along with the local Indian agency headquarters. When that location was deemed not suitable, local tribes sought a new location for a school and the agency headquarters.

A day school was opened on the Puyallup reservation in 1860, near what is now East 29th Street and Portland Avenue in Tacoma. The room was a 16-square-foot, one-room shack with a single door and window. The building was made of rough lumber, constructed with the help of tribal children. Inside the schoolhouse were a few rough benches. Five boys attended the school and studied from a single book. The teacher, whose

Group portrait of students and faculty at the Cushman Indian Trades Industrial Boarding School on the Puyallup Reservation, ca. 1883. The male students are on the left side of the photograph, the female students on the right. Courtesy of the Washington State Historical Society.

Cushman basketball team, 1913. Courtesy of Jane Wright.

Cushman students, early 1900s. Courtesy Ione Knox Collection.

name doesn't survive in records, was a white male. It was only four years before the Tribe realized they needed a new building, though, because serious flooding due to frequent overflowing of the river became a significant problem and kept students from the building for long periods of time.

In the early 1870s, Reverend George W. Sloan came to the reservation to build a permanent boarding school, the Puyallup Indian School. Puyallup Chief Thomas Stoyler, who had cleared land and established an orchard and a home near the Tribe's present-day administration building, donated his land for a school. On Stoyler's site, a new, two-story school building was made of rough lumber. The first floor was a classroom with benches and the second floor was made into a boys' dormitory. In the back of the building were a kitchen and a dining room, and upstairs was a girls' dormitory.

Henry Sicade, who enrolled at the school in 1873 and later recorded his memories of the building, wrote that the boys' quarters were poorly built and inadequately insulated—in winter months the students struggled to perform simple tasks because of the biting temperatures.

Sloan continued to manage the school, and under his tenure about 12 students, including three of his own children, attended the small schoolhouse. Sicade recalled Sloan's kindness and attentiveness to the students and their families. Under his tenure the students learned to read and write, and performed work on the school grounds such as clearing the land and filling in gullies. Upon the death of Sloan's wife the family departed, leaving a school of about 20 students including six or seven girls.

Over the next decade, the school had several teachers stationed on the reservation, and school sessions were often interrupted for weeks or months when teachers left. As Sicade noted, many of the early teachers did not take much interest in students' educational progress. The teachers had varying strategies and views on punishment, and over the years the students were often put to work clearing and farming the land. The students typically spent half a day studying and half a day working, and occasionally spent whole days working. As Sicade recalled, students were often short on clothing and provisions, and those whose parents could not furnish such provisions stocked up on fish from nearby streams. The students' meals typically consisted of some combination of cornmeal, black molasses, and bread, although occasionally they were served stew with potatoes or hardtack in addition.

The school closed briefly in 1875 due to lack of provisions for the students. It was opened a year later with only three students, all boys, who spent most of their days working until a few more students enrolled. Measles swept the small school building, and some students died. The students suffered in the school building without treatment, or even food.

During the decades of the 1860s and 1870s, the Tribe relied on white doctors who came onto the reservation periodically to care for sick children and adults. The diseases of white settlers continued to take a toll on local Indians. While many of the doctors who took up work with the Tribe worked tirelessly to see to the health of tribal members, some were seldom seen on the reservation.

The Tribe's first resident physician, Dr. J.A.C. McCoy, arrived in the late summer of 1878 with his family. McCoy's arrival brought to the school increased good will, previously damaged by ineffective teachers and harsh punishment, and the school continued to grow. Soon, enrollment reached about 50.

McCoy offered older students the opportunity to learn to

Staff of Tacoma Indian Hospital, 1959.

Tacoma Indian Hospital.

A Puyallup Valley Indian hops picker and child were photographed by M.D. True circa 1906. The baby is strapped down in a wooden cradle held in its mother's lap. A makeshift shelter has been erected in the fields with a blanket or tarp providing some protection against the elements. A large basket, in the process of being woven, is on the ground next to the woman. The Puyallup Valley was once home to many hop fields before disease and weather decimated the industry. The Wilhelm Collection. (The Coast magazine June 1906 p.239) Courtesy of the Tacoma Public Library.

In this photograph believed to be from the mid 1880s, a group of Puyallup Indians gathers on the shore of the Puget Sound to gamble. The game they are playing appears to be the Indian bone game, where two teams of 10-12 sit opposite each other. One team has four white bones that they pass to the distracting accompaniment of the pounding of sticks and singing of chants. The other team must guess who has the marked bones. In the background are canoes and a rickety bridge. The Puyallup village during this time period was believed to be at the foot of South 15th Street. Courtesy of the Tacoma Public Library.

Cushman students. Courtesy Ione Knox Collection.

Cushman School Band, date unknown. Courtesy of Jane Wright.

Cushman School Band, date unknown. Courtesy Ione Knox Collection.

roll pills and perform pharmaceutical work. Intermodal athletic competitions were organized among nearly a dozen different local tribes. Morale among students continued to increase.

Following the Civil War, an emerging goal in the Pacific Northwest and around the country among leaders in Indian education strove to assimilate Indian students by placing them in institutions where their cultural practices and language were effectively prohibited. Federal policy called for the removal of children from their families and the placement of those children in government-run schools specifically for this goal. The idea of this policy was to separate the children from cultural and familial influences that U.S. policy makers felt were preventing Native American assimilation into white society.

One of the first Indian boarding schools to implement such policies was the Carlisle Indian School in Pennsylvania, founded by Captain Richard Henry Pratt in 1879. The school was effective at convincing many that such educational practices would benefit Indian students around the country, including in the Northwest.

A school called the Forest Grove Indian School, modeled after Pratt's school and later known as the Chemawa Indian School, opened in 1880 in Forest Grove, Oregon. A total of 18 students from the Puyallup Indian School—14 boys and four girls—were sent to Oregon to continue their education. The students departed in February 1880, and Sicade was among them.

The curriculum and characteristics of Forest Grove, like all federal boarding schools, were closely prescribed by the government. The students followed military-style regimens, strict rules that allowed students to speak only English and an emphasis not only on academics but vocational education. Students typically spent half their day in the classroom and half their day working. Girls learned household tasks such as laundry, sewing and cooking, while boys learned skills such as carpentry and animal husbandry. Students also spent much of their time tending to gardens and livestock, which provided their meals.

The name of the school was changed to Chemawa Indian School in 1885, when it was relocated from Forest Grove to Salem, Oregon. By 1920, the school enrolled more than 900 students from 90 different tribes.

The Puyallup Indian School also felt the effects of the new movement in Indian education in the late 1800s. The school implemented strict policies to eradicate the students' cultural practices and language. During the 1890s, the Puyallup Indian School experienced several changes in leadership and with those, significant changes to the school itself. What was once a small boarding school quickly turned into a large boarding school drawing hundreds of students from the Northwest and Alaska. By 1890 the school had grown to about 200 pupils.

In about 1895, a new principal, Dr. R. E. L. Newberne, took over the school, and invited students from all over the Northwest and Alaska to attend the school. During 1899, under new principal Major Frank Terry, new buildings were constructed on the school grounds—a dining room, a school room and boys' quarters. Terry, who treated members of the Tribe well, was replaced in 1900 by Joseph C. Hart, who terminated or cut the pay of all the school's Indian employees. Attendance again suffered as quarrels and ill-will pervaded. Several tribal members, including Sicade, threatened to sue the school to collect the money made from the purchase of the school, in order to put it into another building. Hart's tenure was followed by that of Harry F. Liston, whose five-year term was most noted for slack rules.

In 1903, as the Puyallup Indian School continued to strug-

Training at Cushman for male students included military instruction. Courtesy Ione Knox Collection.

Cushman male students doing military drills. Cushman girls learning home economics. Courtesy Ione Knox Collection.

Families pose for a photo at Cushman. Courtesy Ione Knox Collection.

Cushman girls basketball team, 1914. Courtesy Ione Knox Collection.

Cushman football teams, c. 1900. Courtesy Ione Knox Collection.

gle with deficiencies, Sicade and his friend William Wilton began pushing for the establishment of a public school on the Puyallup reservation within what is now the city of Fife. Such a school was established and was heavily attended by Puyallup tribal members. The school quickly grew from a one-room schoolhouse to a two-story building. Over the following two decades, enrollment at the Puyallup Indian School significantly increased. Sicade continued to have a profound impact on education in the area, spending more than 25 years on the Board of the Fife School District.

In June 1908, the Office of Indian Affairs ceased operations at the Puyallup Indian School. A complete closure of the school was prevented by Republican Congressman Francis W. Cushman, who fought hard for the preservation of the school, which he believed brought significant economic benefits to the region. A build-up of the school followed, and the school came under the leadership of H. H. Johnson. Under Johnson's tenure, as many as 350 students attended the school, learning various trades. As Sicade recalled, the school was never in better shape than under Liston, who brought the school up to its highest standards. An alumni association was formed, and banquets and gatherings were held annually. Under federal government direction, the school expanded opportunities to place a heavier emphasis on industrial training. In 1910, the school was renamed the Cushman Indian School, in honor of the man who fought to preserve it.

Johnson's term ended when a new political party forced him out in 1913. He was replaced by T. B. Wilson, whose tenure led to the steadily deteriorating conditions at the school. The years following were marked by a decrease in enrollment, as Puyallup students began attending public schools. The school was closed in the spring of 1917 due to lack of funds. In 1920, the Cushman Indian School was closed for good.

During the 60 years of its existence, the Puyallup Indian School was plagued by political and religious bickering, incompetent or indifferent teachers, poor nutrition and health care for the students and inadequate school infrastructure. In Sicade's writings about his time at the school, he recalls the repeated failure of the school's administration to meet students' needs, and the disillusionment that followed.

Another institution educating Puyallup Indians prevailed, however. Beginning in the mid-1800s, missionaries began building schools for the education of Indian children around the Puget Sound region. Father Peter Hylebos, with the support of the Catholic Church, established the St. George's Indian Mission in 1888. Hylebos, who long took an interest in Indian welfare, previously worked in Washington, D.C. on the Indian Commission of the Catholic Indian Bureau. Hylebos helped negotiate an amicable settlement between the U.S. government and Catholic leaders running Indian schools around the country. In the late 1880s the Catholic Church, noting the problems that plagued the Puyallup Indian School and other institutions, was seeking a more effective—and more religious—education for Indian children in the Puget Sound region. Hylebos, convinced of the need, headed out to the Puyallup reservation to begin work on a new school. Using funding from a wealthy donor and the U.S. government, Hylebos purchased 142 acres of land just north of what is now the Pierce County/King County line. He constructed one large and several smaller buildings for his school, hired six teachers, and officially opened it on October 26, 1888. The opening of the school initiated tensions between St. George's and the Puyallup Indian School, as some students

A group of Puyallup boys and girls, three nuns wearing habits, a priest, and a few men stand outside the large three-storey St. George's Industrial School building in Milton, Wash., 1889. Some children hold farm tools, including a plow, hoe, and whisk broom. Courtesy of the Washington State Historical Society.

Old Ezra Meeker hop yard, Puyallup. View of hops harvesting camp site in Puyallup, ca. 1886-1890. Many tents and large crowds of people (both European and Native American), a British flag and the hops field are visible in the distance. Courtesy of the Washington State Historical Society.

Indian cemetery. This was the Puyallup Indian cemetery located next to the Cushman Veterans Hospital, 2002 E. 28th St., as pictured in May of 1925. Indians under the direction of Henry Sicade of Fife had spent the month cleaning and renovating the old cemetery. They graded, sown grass seed, planted new shrubs, installed a 600-foot wire fence, repaired 300-feet of old fence, and erected 500 marble monuments. Sicade had secured a $3,000 appropriation from the U.S. government for the complete renovation and restoration of the cemetery. There were about 2,000 graves but many had been obliterated. Among those buried there were Chief Salatat, Chief Thomas Stolyer, Chief Sitwell, Chief Tommy Lane and Chief Leschi. The low-lying white fences that surrounded the tribal cemetery have since been replaced by high stone walls. The small church next door was a Presbyterian mission founded in 1881 and since rebuilt. The Cushman Veterans (later Tacoma Indian Hospital) Hospital has been demolished. Courtesy of the Tacoma Public Library.

from the reservation school transferred to Hylebos' mission school.

Parents who wished to send their children to St. George's Catholic School rather than the Puyallup Indian School were dealt with severely by U.S. Indian Agent Edwin Eells and law enforcement. Father Hylebos, resident pastor at St. George's, wanted the school to be a place where Catholic Indians could freely send their children. However, several of the Indians who did so were arrested, including a widowed Indian woman whom Father Hylebos said was kept in the prison on the Puyallup Reservation for the several days it took two of Eells' policemen to arrest her children and take them to the Puyallup Indian School. Another Puyallup Indian, Louis Laclair, was imprisoned the day he took his children to St. George's and many other parents were threatened with the same. Father Hylebos told of how Eells' policemen would visit the homes of Indian Catholics and threaten them with arrest and jail if they sent their children to St. George's. Father Hylebos intervened on Laclair's behalf and the man was released from prison. Father Hylebos testified to all of this and more to Hon. T. J. Morgan, Commissioner of Indian Affairs in Washington, D.C., who didn't believe the priest and told him to "let bygones be bygones." In what could be interpreted as retaliation, Father Hylebos' application to the Commission of Indian Affairs for additional students to enter St. George's was denied along with requests for funding assistance.

Hylebos and the school's first superintendent, Reverend Charles de Decker, closely modeled the curriculum at St. George's with that of the U.S. government schools, incorporating industrial training and domestic skills. The students were also instructed in religion. The children were separated from

St. George's Industrial School. Courtesy of the Washington State Historical Society.

Cushman basketball team. Courtesy of Jane Wright.

Cushman football team, date unknown. Courtesy of Jane Wright.

Cushman girls baseball team, date unknown. Courtesy of Jane Wright.

their families and prohibited from speaking their own language or continuing cultural practices. The school provided accommodations for both day and boarding students. The capacity of the school was 80, and for most of its existence St. George's met that capacity. At some points in its history the school also accepted white and black students in addition to Indian students. The school accepted students ages six through 16 and educated them through age 18.

When the Great Depression hit St. George's had difficulty raising money to maintain operations. The construction of public schools in the area also drew many students out of mission schools. The school at St. George's Indian Mission closed in 1936. The last of the school buildings were razed in 1971.

There would not be a local school specifically for the education of Native American children until 1976, when the Puyallup Tribal School was founded to address the drop-out rate of youth in the Puyallup Tribe. The school first operated in the building of Hawthorne Elementary School, borrowed from the Tacoma School District, at the site of what is now the Tacoma Dome.

In 1978, a new elementary school was built on tribal lands, and middle and high school students were educated in the Tribe's administration building. Soon after, the middle and high school students were relocated to a vacant elementary school on South 72nd Street.

Trying times continued to plague the school, however. By 1983, fewer than 100 students were enrolled in the school, which was threatened with closure as enrollment rates continued to decline. But tribal leaders and others fought to secure money and support for Indian education. With the help of Congressman Norm Dicks, the Tribe secured federal funding, purchased 68 acres of farmland and built Chief Leschi School. Today,

Cushman dining hall, 1914. Courtesy Ione Knox Collection.

Many dances were held at Cushman in the early 1900s. Courtesy Ione Knox Collection.

Cushman football teams, c. 1900. Courtesy Ione Knox Collection.

the school is the largest of seven tribal schools in the state of Washington and one of the most renowned in the country. The school serves approximately 900 students, of which 98 percent are Native American and who represent more than 60 Native American tribes and bands from across the United States.

In 1993 the Puyallup Tribe established a private two-year college, the Medicine Creek Tribal College, located on the Puyallup Indian Reservation in Tacoma. While the school is now closed, it was originally created out of a desire among tribal members to exercise their sovereign rights; the Tribe desired to educate and train Native Americans in the South Puget Sound region. The school provided continuing education to graduates of Chief Leschi school and to other Native Americans seeking higher education, and formed an agreement with Pierce College in Lakewood to develop and offer courses specifically for Native students.

Shortly after the Cushman School closed in 1920, the United States government turned the buildings into a Veterans Administration hospital for soldiers suffering from mental and physical ailments after World War I. The hospital, called The United States Public Health Hospital No. 59, housed 200 veterans. A new neuropsychiatric ward, announced in 1921, would house an additional 140 patients. The new ward would also house more than 100 tuberculosis patients.

By the end of 1921, significant work and money had been put into the former school to house disabled veterans and other patients. In October 1921, about a year after the hospital began accepting patients, there were a total of 42 buildings and 242 patients. Staff included 10 medical officers, one dentist, 45 nurses and orderlies, two dietitians, three occupational therapy aides, five physiotherapy aides and three vocational education

Cushman basketball team, 1913. Courtesy of Jane Wright.

Cushman basketball team, 1917. Courtesy of Jane Wright.

Cushman students, early 1900s. Courtesy Ione Knox Collection.

Formal group portrait of students at the Cushman Indian Trades School, 1891. Dressed in European style clothing, the women are seated in the front row and the men are standing behind them. There are a few houses in the background. Courtesy of the Washington State Historical Society.

teachers.

Shortly thereafter, the U.S. Department of Veterans Affairs announced the opening of a hospital on American Lake to serve World War I veterans in need of neuropsychiatric treatment in 1923. On November 21 of that year, the U.S. government announced the closure of the Cushman Hospital in 1928, and ordered that no more patients be received. In response, many patients and the American Legion fought to maintain the hospital as a permanent institution. Those who fought against the closure argued that the new facility at American Lake was not as good as the Cushman Hospital. In response, the Department of Veterans Affairs argued that Cushman was a fire hazard because 39 of the buildings had wood frames.

The battle raged for several years until, in 1927, the Department of Veterans Affairs abandoned plans to close Cushman Hospital in 1928, and restructured the nature of the American Lake facility to meet its needs. The decision was short-lived, however. A year later, in December 1928, the VA announced that no more patients would be accepted, and would instead be diverted to a hospital in Portland.

Cushman Hospital was given new life almost immediately however, when control was returned to the Bureau of Indian Affairs. The hospital closed to veterans on January 15, 1929, and reopened six months later under the supervision of Dr. John N. Alley, as a facility to treat Indians from Washington, Oregon, and northern California suffering from tuberculosis. Local residents protested the change, but it nonetheless opened in July 1929. In the first year of its operations, agents with the BIA brought in more than 700 Indians for treatment, most of whom were children. In June 1930, there were more than 200 patients in the hospital, and the children received education

Cushman basketball players. Courtesy Ione Knox Collection.

The 1929 Puyallup Tribal Membership Enrollment Committee. Back row, left to right: William Wilton, Benjamin Wright; Front row, left to right: Henry Sicade, Jerry Meeker and Silas Cross. Courtesy Cross Collection.

Learning industrial trades at Cushman School. Courtesy Ione Knox Collection.

Cushman students, c. 1900. Courtesy Ione Knox Collection.

through eighth grade from a staff of three teachers.

In May 1931 Puyallup tribal members voted to sell the Cushman Hospital to the U.S. government, which had been paying an annual rent of $9,000 on the land. The selling price was around $400,000, which was to be divided equally among the 340 tribal members. The primary purpose of the agreement was to allow for the building of additional facilities on the 33-acre campus, and the government would not commence construction unless they held title to the land, therefore forcing the Tribe to sell the site to the government.

The U.S. Congress, however, failed to appropriate the funds to purchase the land. Tribal members continued to pressure the U.S. government over the coming years, and lost out on significant opportunities for improvement because the United States was not in possession of the land. In their proposals to Congress, tribal members and their supporters argued that the buildings needed to be updated, as they were far below the minimum standards for medical services. The danger of fire continued to be a concern that many felt needed to be addressed. Still, the U.S. Congress failed to appropriate funds to purchase or improve the facility.

In 1938 a supply building at the hospital was destroyed by fire, but other buildings were saved. Damage to the building was estimated to be about $5,000 and loss of property within the building was estimated at $25,000. Finally in August 1939, President Franklin Roosevelt signed a bill to purchase the site. Congressman John Coffee, who sponsored the bill, said the purchase meant the facility would receive extensive renovations and new permanent fireproof buildings on the site.

In 1941 the site received the promised renovations. In that year the U.S. government announced $1.7 million in major

Cushman students, c. 1900. Courtesy Ione Knox Collection.

renovations and additions, including a new six-story hospital building made of fireproof brick and tile over reinforced concrete. The hospital was completed in April 1943, and was called by the Tacoma News Tribune "one of America's great medical centers." The center included facilities for general medical treatment, surgery, orthopedic treatment, X-ray and tubercular and obstetrical cases. It came to be known as the largest Indian medical center in the United States.

In July 1954 the Department of the Interior announced that responsibility for furnishing the care provided at the hospital would be transferred from the Bureau of Indian Affairs to local agencies, and would place a renewed emphasis on treating tuberculosis patients from around the Northwest. By the end of the year the hospital transitioned to a facility exclusively to treat tuberculosis. Staff levels were reduced by between 15 and 20 percent. By January 1, 1955, the hospital was converted entirely to a tuberculosis sanatorium. The sanatorium soon fell under the direction of the U.S. Public Health Service. By 1956, five doctors were caring for about 270 patients a day.

As tuberculosis cases declined, the hospital continued to see fewer patients. In January 1959 it was reported that the hospital saw a decrease in patient load of about 35 percent, from 285 cases to 161. A decision of whether to close the sanatorium fell to the U.S. Department of Health, Welfare and Education. In March 1959, Indians from local tribes and tribes as far away as Minnesota and Oklahoma formally protested the closing of the facility. Congressman Coffee, long a supporter of the hospital, also protested the closure. Nevertheless, hearings were set in Washington, D.C. to consider closure of the facility.

In July 1959 the Department of Health, Education and Welfare officially announced plans to close down the Cushman

Hospital on September 15 of that same year. The hospital was closed, and many tribal members working at the hospital lost their jobs. In 1960 the site was declared surplus property. The state of Washington stepped in and applied for transfer of the property to be used as a diagnostic and treatment center for children who were admitted to the Washington State Department of Institutions by the state's juvenile court system. An agreement was executed in 1961 that allowed the state of Washington to retain use of the site for 20 years. The state began phasing out the juvenile program in the late 1970s.

Following the closure of the Cushman Hospital in 1959, only dental care services were provided to members of the Puyallup Tribe in the form of a mobile trailer parked in the tribal cemetery. Problems regarding eligibility, fee schedules and billing procedures made it difficult for many members to gain access to quality care. Insufficient funds only contributed to the obstacles facing tribal members.

To seek better solutions for its members, the tribal council appointed an Education and Health Committee. Shortly thereafter, in 1974, the Tribe received funds for a medical clinic. For a decade tribal members received care from a double-wide modular. But in 1985, it became clear that the small building could not accommodate the growing population of Native Americans in Pierce County, so the Tribe began work on what is now the Puyallup Tribal Health Authority (PTHA). The 43,000-square-foot facility was completed in 1993. It is owned by the Indian Health Service and operated by the Puyallup Tribe.

Today the PTHA treats more than 10,000 patients representing 120 different tribes every year. The clinic, open five days a week, provides dental care, X-ray services, a pharmacy, mental health care, nutrition, traditional healing and other services.

CHAPTER 5

GOVERNMENTAL ORGANIZATION OF THE PUYALLUP TRIBE

During the about eight decades following the signing of the Medicine Creek Treaty, tribal members became increasingly disenfranchised as they lost even more land dedicated for their use through the treaty. Allotments and tribal lands were literally taken from the hands of tribal members, and their rights as sovereign people and values as a distinct culture had been impeded through the end of the 19th century and into the 20th.

In the late 1920s the Puyallup Tribe began to take steps to officially re-form its membership, policies, and stance in the non-tribal world. The membership roll of 1929; the federal Indian Reorganization Act of 1934, also known as the Wheeler-Howard Act; and the creation of a federally recognized government and constitution paved the way for the action toward increased independence for the Tribe.

In February 1926, Puyallup tribal members held a meeting

discussing the sale of tribal lands. Payment of the property would be divided among tribal members as a per capita payment, which meant the Tribe needed to determine how many members it had and who they were.

The property to be sold included land at the old Cushman School and about 30 lots adjacent to the area. At the time, the school was being used as a veterans hospital. In August 1939, after the Tribe made several attempts to transfer title of the Cushman site to the United States, the area finally changed hands from the Tribe's ownership to the federal government's. It provided $228,525, divided among the roll established ten years earlier, which stated there were 340 tribal members in 1929.

WHEELER-HOWARD ACT

In the 1930s tribes across the country were given the opportunity to regain land and formalize governments that would finally put them in a position to officially control their own affairs and begin to make a name for themselves as viable, respected governing bodies and nations.

The Indian Reorganization Act of 1934, also referred to as the Wheeler-Howard Act, gave tribes the right to self-govern and allowed them to manage their own land and assets. The act was intended to create self-sufficiency for tribes as well by attempting to establish strong economic bases for reservations.

The Indian Reorganization Act allowed the Puyallup Tribe to take a stake in their future, solidify a government, and begin to start re-acquiring lands they had lost decades before, although the first lands regained by tribal members did not occur for more than 40 years.

Before the Indian Reorganization Act, under which many tribes adopted federally recognized constitutions and councils, the Puyallup Tribe had been led by elected leaders, often well-known and influential tribal members. While at the time of the treaty negotiations, representative leaders, or chiefs, were designated by territorial officials, several prominent tribal leaders can be noted for the Puyallup Tribe.

In 1856 in a letter written by Indian Agent Wesley B. Gosnell, he noted that the chief of the Puyallup Tribe, K'Qatch-ee, had died and that the new head of the Tribe was Es-ahl-atahtl. An excerpt from Herbert Hunt's "History of Tacoma" relays a succession of chief leaders who may have carried the Tribe into the 1900s. "The Puyallup chiefs from Squatahan's time—in the (1850s)—were 'Tyee Dick,' whose Indian name was Sinawah; then Sitwell, whose correct name was Sitwulch and who had a great influence; the fourth was Tom Thompson, whose Indian name was Za-qua-la-oc. Sitwell then served for another period as leader of the Tribe, being followed by Quayupyet, generally known as Tommy Lane." A man highly thought of, Lane is fondly and respectfully remembered today for everything he did for the Puyallups as their chief leader.

In 1872 General Milory, superintendent of Indian Affairs, required an annual election of chiefs, a practice the Tribe had always done, simply without the many formalities imposed by the white governments. Tribal elections were often delayed as the Indians discussed the merits of the candidates before they were put up for a vote of the membership.

Shortly prior to the formation of tribal councils under the Indian Reorganization Act, minutes from membership meetings show that a council-style of government was already used. Although the Tribe had officially been recognized since the Treaty of Medicine Creek, the Indian Reorganization Act authorized the creation of an official Tribal government and Tribal constitution.

In 1936 the Puyallup Tribe elected its first council of five people. Shortly after, the council signed the constitution and Bylaws for the Puyallup Tribe, a document written and established by the Bureau of Indian Affairs. The constitution, which was very similar to the 100 or so other constitutions signed by tribes under the Act, outlined membership eligibility, council roles and responsibilities, a bill of rights and tribal land rights, rules and restrictions.

Puyallup Tribe's Bill of Rights:

1. All members 18 years and older can vote (amendment made in 1991).

2. Economic rights: All members of the Tribe shall be accorded equal opportunities to participate in the economic resources and activities of the Tribe.

3. Civil liberties: All members of the Tribe may enjoy without hindrance freedom of worship, conscience, speech, press, assembly, and association.

4. Rights of accused: Any members of the Tribe accused of any offense shall have the right to a prompt, open, and public hearing, with due notice of offense charged, and shall be permitted to summon witnesses on his own behalf. Trial by jury may be demanded of any offense punishable by more than 30 days imprisonment. Excessive bail shall not be required, and cruel punishment shall not be imposed."

The Constitutions and Bylaws of the Puyallup Tribe of Indians was approved on March 11, 1936 by the Secretary of the Interior Harold J. Ickes. On April 11, 1936 it was ratified by a vote of the Puyallup tribal membership, with 55 for and 15 against in an election in which more than 30 percent of eligible voters voted.

The Puyallup Tribe's constitution has been amended three times since its ratification in 1936. In 1970 eligibility of membership was altered. The constitution had previously stated that all members must have been listed on the membership roll of 1929, or children born to those on the membership roll, and residing on the reservation or within 20 miles of the Tacoma Hospital Center. The 1970 amendments changed eligibility requirements to include any child born to a person of the Tribe, with no residential requirements. It also changed qualifications for members to run for the tribal council. Before 1970 Puyallup tribal members could not run for council unless they resided in the same 20-mile radius of the Tacoma Hospital Center and reservation for at least one year. The amendment eliminated the residency requirement for council members and also changed the stipulations of termination proceedings due to the death, resignation, or felony conviction of a council member. Previously, a council member's term would be ended if he/she moved off the reservation.

The main change made in 1991 was language to prohibit dual enrollment for members. Changes in 1991 also eliminated the requirement of the council to get approval from the Bureau of Indian Affairs on council action, and increased the council from five to seven members.

The voting age was also reduced from 21 to 18 for tribal members. The latest amendment was made in 2005 and was spurred by the implementation of the large per capita payments enacted by council in 2002. The constitution was amended to prohibit people from transferring into the Tribe later in life in order to receive the benefits. Puyallup tribal members now must be enrolled within one year of birth.

In addition to establishing tribal governments and constitutions, the Indian Reorganization Act also intended to reverse the extreme loss of Indian land. The Act authorized the Department of the Interior to reacquire land for the Indians and put it into a trust status, a process that was also created through the Act. Land acquisition on behalf of the Tribe happened slowly at first. The first instances of the Department of the Interior putting tribal lands into trust occurred four decades after the establishment of the Act.

In 1977 a lawsuit was filed by the City of Tacoma against Secretary of the Interior Cecil Andrus. This was one of the first, if not the first, instances of the department putting Puyallup tribal lands into trust, and the city fought the bureau, as well as the Tribe, for lands they believed should not be put back into the hands of the Puyallup people.

The lawsuit pertained to tracts of land that had been put into trust at the request of the Tribe as well as individual tribal members. The tracts were laid out in several areas throughout the reservation and, when put back into trust, would decrease the city's property tax roll, as well as diminish its jurisdiction. The city argued that while the Indian Reorganization Act of 1934 authorized taking land into trust, it did not authorize the acquisitions of the parcels for tribal members. The lawsuit lasted a little over one year and during that time froze all other land acquisitions on behalf of the Tribe. A judge ruled in favor of the Tribe and the Department of the Interior, stating that being able to take all tribal lands back into trust was the exact reason the Indian Reorganization Act was established.

During this time in the mid-to-late 1970s the Tribe was just beginning to reassert itself. Milestone events such as the Fishing Wars, the takeover of Cascadia Diagnostics Center, and establishment of the health authority would all give validity to the

Tribe's name and reputation. While it took several decades for the Tribe to go after their land under the Reorganization Act, the timing of the first acquisitions in 1977 was fitting. Since then only a few acres have been put into trust on behalf of the Tribe. The Land Claims Settlement of 1988 was a huge feat for the Tribe, as surrounding jurisdictions returned 900 acres to the Tribe.

A STORY OF OUR MOUNTAIN

"Before the world changed, five sisters lived where Orting is now," recalled Jerry Meeker, a Puyallup, ninety years old in 1952. "When Doquebuth the Changer came, he changed them into five mountains. One of them was called Takkobad by my people. That is Mount Rainier. I forgot the Indian names for the other sisters – Mount Baker, Mount Adams, Mount St. Helens, and Mount Hood.

"Doquebuth said to Takkobad, 'You will take care of the Sound country. You will supply the water. You will be useful in that way.' 'Ko mean 'water'" added Mr. Meeker.
In the summer of 1900, a nephew of Chief Seattle told another story about the original name of Mount Rainier, as he sat looking at it from Longmire Springs. It also is said to be a Puyallup myth.

"When Doklbahl (the Changer of all things) saw that his work was done, he went and sat on a high mountain. From this he gazed upon his work and then said to the mountain, "You shall be Ta-ko-bid, because upon you I have rested and you are so near the Divine."

"Indian Legends of the Pacific Northwest"
by Ella Clark, as told by Jerry Meeker

The Northwest's Original
BROWNS POINT SALMON BAKE
Saturday and Sunday August 4-5, 1962

Photo by Lorenzo da Ponte

JERRY MEEKER, 1862-1955
Beloved Indian First Citizen of Browns Point,
Originator and Guiding Hand of The Salmon Bakes

★ ★ ★

SPONSORED BY
BROWN'S POINT IMPROVEMENT CLUB
BROWNS POINT, WASHINGTON

CHAPTER 6

FISHING RIGHTS STRUGGLE

Perhaps the most critical struggle to face the Puyallup Tribe erupted over their right to fish the waters of their homeland. Efforts to impede, and stop, Pacific Coast tribes from fishing have been underway for many decades, despite the fact that tribal fishing rights have been guaranteed since 1855 by the federal government upon the ratification of the Medicine Creek Treaty. Article III states:

> "The right of taking fish at all usual and accustomed grounds and stations is further secured to said Indians in common with all citizens of the Territory, and of erecting temporary houses for the purpose of curing, together with the privilege of hunting, gathering roots and berries, and pasturing their horses on open and unclaimed lands: Provided, however, that they shall not take shellfish from any beds staked or cultivated by

Yelm Jim tends to his fish weir on Wapato Creek on the Puyallup Reservation, a method of trapping fish used by the Puyallups for many generations.

Puyallup Tribal member Don McCloud fishes on the Nisqually River.

citizens...."

The language in the treaty sounds direct and explicit, yet despite what the federal government promised to Northwest Indian tribes in signed treaties, conflicts remained in Washington state over tribal fishing. The Puyallup and other treaty tribes have spent 150 years defending that right on the waters of western Washington and in courtrooms across the country. Struggling against efforts to stop them, Puyallup tribal fishermen and fishermen of other local tribes continued to fish in their usual and accustomed places to fulfill numerous necessities including feeding their own families and making an income. Tribal fishermen used fish as a trade item with local whites and with tribes from eastern Washington that would travel west for many miles to get valuable and delicious salmon. In later years, fishmongers bought fish from the tribal fisheries, and families could fetch a decent price in the sale.

As non-Indian sport and commercial fishing industries increased during the second half of the 19th century, the beginning of a long and drawn-out fishing battle was also at hand. To regulate these industries, the state of Washington established the Department of Fisheries in 1891, and in 1899 it became the Department of Fisheries and Game. In the early 1930s the department was split into two separate entities.

Although the Medicine Creek Treaty clearly gives the Puyallup Indians the right to fish, the state increased its regulation of fishing over the years, and in 1973 made gillnetting in rivers illegal. Some Puyallup fishermen continued to net-fish according to their treaty rights, but at their own risk. Commercial and sport fishermen grew agitated at the tribal fisheries, and game wardens routinely arrested Indian fishermen and confiscated their gear.

By the first half of the 20th century, fishing by tribal members was so vigorously prohibited and so many tribal fishermen were prosecuted that it almost brought fishing by tribal members to a halt. Decades after the Medicine Creek Treaty was signed, a full political movement to address the fishing rights issue began to coalesce among some members of local tribes and their supporters. The "Fishing Wars," as the movement came to be called, escalated in the 1960s and reached a fever pitch in the early 1970s. Similarly during these years, other "people's movements" were grabbing headlines—the Puyallup Tribe's fight for their treaty rights reflected what was going on across the country in terms of political and social movements for change, including the national American Indian Movement (AIM), the civil rights movement, the women's rights movement, and the Vietnam War protests, among numerous others. The rallying song "We Shall Overcome" became a clarion call from coast to coast for minorities and women who wanted a better life, and the sentiment resonated with the Puyallup Tribe as well.

It's important to note that the fishing rights movement was not supported by all Tribal members. Some saw it as too radical, an argument common in grassroots political movements over whether civil disobedience is the right way to affect change. But others believed that drastic times called for drastic measures, and they were determined to succeed.

As Puyallup fishermen held with all their might onto one of the last remaining vestiges of their traditional livelihood, the state of Washington, commercial fisheries, sport fishermen, and emboldened individual citizens formed a formidable wall against the tribal fisheries. However, a group of committed Puyallup Indians and their supporters built an armed encampment on the Puyallup riverbank to defend tribal fishermen, and

Local law enforcement kept a close eye on the encampment day and night. Despite tribal members' pledge of nonviolence, officers from Tacoma Police Department are seen here aiming a telescopic rifle at the camp as if ready to shoot at any moment. Courtesy of Daniel Fear.

held protests like "fish-ins" to expose attacks they suffered while fishing on the banks of their own homes.

In the Courtrooms

There has been a steady stream of lawsuits addressing the Tribe's treaty fishing rights ever since Washington became a state. At the time the lawsuits were being filed, the Puyallup Tribe was living in poverty. Tribal families were barely making ends meet with meager incomes, yet considerable amounts of money were required for the Tribe to cover its legal expenses. This put major hardships on the people whose fishing rights were already plainly spelled out in the Medicine Creek Treaty.

The United States Supreme Court decided several cases through the first half of the 20th century that generally supported and upheld the Tribe's treaty rights but that did not prevent the state and its enforcement agencies from arresting Tribal members and trying to prevent them from fishing.

Although the Puyallup Tribe, its members and its lawyers have been fighting for the Tribe's fishing rights in countless courtrooms, two cases in particular have shaped the legal principles controlling treaty fishing rights. One, *Washington State Department of Game v. Puyallup Tribe*, was in the courts for 17 years, including three trips to the United States Supreme Court. The other, *United States v. Washington*, has been in federal court for 40 years and continues to move forward in courtrooms to this day.

In 1963 the state of Washington filed *Washington State Department of Game v. Puyallup Tribe*. It began as a series of state court criminal prosecutions against tribal members for fishing with nets for steelhead in violation of state fishing regulations. Tribal members had fished like that for millennia, but

Washington state law reserved steelhead for the hook-and-line sport fishery. The main goal for the state was to prevent the Puyallups from exercising any "special" Indian fishing rights, specifically the use of gillnets to catch steelhead trout, either on or off the reservation. It took three trips to the U.S. Supreme Court to settle the suit.

Two years later the battle took a critical turn when a Pierce County Superior Court ruling prohibited Indians from net fishing on certain sections of the Nisqually and Puyallup rivers. It was also during this time that the Puyallup Tribe's very existence came into question in the courts, making tribal activists both angry and more determined than ever to defend their Tribe. In May 1965, Judge John D. Cochran of Pierce County Superior Court ruled that the Puyallup Tribe didn't really exist, and issued a permanent injunction against Puyallup Indians fishing in the Puyallup River.

The Puyallup Tribe was very poor financially during this point in its history, and rulings like Cochran's added more hardship to their suffering. All throughout the decades that the Puyallup Tribe defended itself in court, much effort was put into raising money for expenses such as attorneys' fees, travel to Washington, D.C., document preparation, and other legal costs. Somehow the Tribe managed, but it was no easy road.

The U.S. Supreme Court issued a ruling in *Washington State Department of Game v. Puyallup Tribe* in 1968. Given the label "Puyallup I," the Court ruled: "The right to fish 'at all usual and accustomed' places may... not be qualified by the State...." The Court went on to rule, however, that the state could regulate the way in which tribal members fished if those measures were "reasonable and necessary for conservation," to preserve the species from extinction. That phrase became the guiding principle for state regulation of treaty fishing rights.

Frank's Landing

On the water, the situation had grown dire by this point. State game wardens and law enforcement were getting more brazen in their attacks on Native fishermen and their families. This is well illustrated in accounts of what occurred at Frank's Landing on the Nisqually Indian Reservation, situated on the Nisqually River about 20 miles south of Puyallup territory. The story of the Puyallup Tribe's involvement in the Fishing Wars can't be told without including the story of Frank's Landing, the epicenter of the Nisqually Tribe's fishing wars, and their involvement directly affected the Puyallup Tribe, just as the Puyallup's battles impacted the nearby Nisqually.

Named for Billy Frank, Sr., whose extended family lived on the river shores and fished together for generations, Frank's Landing was under round-the-clock surveillance by law enforcement authorities. Whenever Native fishermen at the Landing set nets in the water, on the opposite bank of the river game wardens sat in their trucks watching and ready to descend upon the tribal boats. Law enforcement officers would routinely seize the Indians' nets and gear right out from their own hands. Fist fights broke out, and the Indian children witnessed this violence being rained down upon their moms and dads, aunts, uncles and grandparents.

Many Indians who fished on the Nisqually River were arrested, some many times, and families would pawn valuable items like boat motors for bail money. Already facing financial hardship from being denied the right to fish, it was hard for the fishermen to replace their gear. Without being allowed to fish, families that relied on the income from selling their catch were left in poverty. Fathers taken to jail couldn't support their wives and children, let alone access money for bail and attorney fees. State wardens were openly taking canoes and fishing gear, and more thieves would join them under the cover of night. With no money to purchase new gear, the situation for tribal families became all the more serious.

This account from the late Alison Gottfriedson, who lived at Frank's Landing, describes life at the Landing and the day that state law enforcement officers commenced what became known as the Battle of Frank's Landing. A former Puyallup Tribal Council member, an activist for treaty rights and fishing rights, and a strong voice for women's leadership in the Tribe, Alison was just a teenager at this time.

"I would wake up during the night and see my mother standing at the window, watching for my dad. There would be huge spotlights across the river. Whether on shore or on wardens' boats, the lights would shine up and down the river, looking for my dad and other fishermen. Sometimes he made it home; sometimes he didn't.

"I remember as a child feeling scared and worried—not knowing what was going to happen to my parents. The clashes began to get more violent. I was drawn into that violence when I was 13 years old. That was the first time I was involved in a full-blown riot. With a force of 250 strong, the state came in on us (about 25-30 Indians, mostly women and children), on October 13, 1965, arresting eight men and women including my mom and dad. And they came in clubbing and striking with billyclubs, eight-cell flashlights and brass knuckles. I watched as they clubbed and beat people. I watched them while they clubbed my dad, handcuffed him, hit him on the back with brass knuckles, and yanked his arm high up his back! I also watched

To show solidarity with the Puyallup Tribe in its fight for fishing rights, members of the Black Panther Party added their welcomed presence to the riverside encampment. Courtesy of Daniel Fear.

On the day authorities raided the Puyallup's encampment, fire broke out on the Puyallup River bridge train trestle, sending billows of black, acrid smoke into the air. Courtesy of Daniel Fear.

them take my mom down, twisting her arms up her back and forcefully hitting her!

"I was standing beside my 14-year-old sister, Valerie, when a game warden grabbed me by the hair and tried to pound my head into a huge log that was sticking out of the water. My sister then started fighting with him, trying to make him let go of my hair. He turned to her and punched her in the face! Her nose started bleeding and quickly she had blood all over her face and the front of her shirt. I saw the other Indian children, in terror, watching their families being beaten and drug off to jail."

As the Fishing Wars became more heated and the abuse of the Native American fishermen greater, members of various tribes at Frank's Landing formed the Survival of the American Indians Association. The group fought for the Tribe's treaty rights, and brainstormed strategies to retain those rights including hiring attorneys. Young people were especially important to the association to help guard the Tribe's boats 24 hours a day.

Frank's Landing inspired some Puyallup Indians to take a firm stand of their own by setting up an armed encampment on the Puyallup River. The camp captured public attention quickly, and news reporters milled around with photographers to get the latest scoop. Clashes with law enforcement were common. Far outnumbering the tribal peoples and their many supporters, police and game wardens showed themselves to be a brutal muscle for the state. Sympathizers representing a rainbow of colors and cultures came to the Puyallup camp. Through with seeing tribal fishermen being beaten and arrested by authorities, many Puyallup tribal members became full-time activists.

By the late 1960s organized protests were common at the state capitol in Olympia. At one key media event, tribal fishermen dropped their nets into the water at the mouth of the Capitol

Lake Dam in Olympia to the consternation of law enforcement officers. The activists planned this demonstration to show the public in broad daylight the type of actions that were taking place under cover of night on the rivers. As cameras were rolling, officers roared in as predicted and pulled up the nets. Fights broke out as tribal members tried to defend themselves. Onlookers watched in shock as seven demonstrators were arrested and dragged away. The spectacle delivered another serious blow to the state, which was having an increasingly difficult time defending its wholesale policies against tribal fishing.

More publicity came when celebrities came to add the weight of their stardom to the fight. Acclaimed movie star Marlon Brando was the first to come, one of the few non-Natives of that era who listened to the Indians and publicly stepped up to defend their right to fish. Jane Fonda also traveled to the Northwest to lend her support. Another noted visitor was Native American activist, educator, Academy Award-winning songwriter and performer Buffy Sainte-Marie, who blessed everyone with her strong and gentle presence.

African American civil rights activist and comedic entertainer Dick Gregory net-fished on the Nisqually River in 1968, was arrested and sentenced to serve 90 days in Thurston County Jail. He went on a hunger strike while incarcerated, pledging to live only on bread and distilled water until his release. About six weeks later he became ill and was hospitalized, then ultimately sent to his home in Chicago to finish out his sentence. An outspoken activist in support of many struggles, Gregory's rich history of speaking and acting against injustice made him not only a hero among movement leaders across the country, but also earned him more than 45,000 votes when he ran for U.S. President in the late 1960s as a write-in candidate of the

The Puyallup Tribe's encampment on the Puyallup River brought much needed attention to the Tribe's fight for its fishing rights. Members of other tribes came to help too, especially the Nisqually. Here, Nisqually fishing rights leader Al Bridges speaks through a bullhorn. In the foreground are Puyallup tribal men and ardent fishing rights defenders Charlie Cantrell (with hands on hips) and Silas "Boo" Cross (next to him in hat). Courtesy of Andy De Los Angeles.

Freedom and Peace Party. His attention to the fishing struggle of Northwest Indians was most welcomed by those tribal members who knew the publicity would only help draw additional attention to their fight.

At the Puyallup encampment the air remained tense and determined. Law enforcement maintained a presence in greater numbers and with more firepower than in the tribal people's arsenal. Spontaneous police raids failed to break up the encampment, but the pressure never receded. The activists and their supporters stood their ground, with security patrols day and night. Tribal members from across the country came to support their brothers and sisters—Yakama, Cree, Blackfoot, Sioux, and Cherokee among many others. Activists from other civil rights movements came as well to create a united front, including members of the Black Panthers.

The standoff seemed interminable, until September 9, 1970. Police with tear gas and state game officers with clubs raided the encampment that day at dawn. Shots were fired and police sent the riot squad in. A group of Indian activists tried to defend themselves from the onslaught on the Milwaukee Road Bridge over the Puyallup River, but they were forced to flee when it suddenly caught fire. Plumes of black smoke smeared the sky, creating an ominous vision. Local news reported that nearly 60 were arrested that day and charged with rioting; the charges were later dropped. A few days later, the United States Attorney General at long last filed *United States v. Washington*, a major lawsuit designed to protect the treaty fishing rights of tribes in Western Washington. *United States v. Washington* wound its way through the court system for four years before a ruling was made, but that didn't end the suit, which is coming up on its 40th anniversary.

Back in the Courtrooms

While *Washington State Department of Game v. Puyallup Tribe* was going back and forth from the state courts to the U.S. Supreme Court following the ruling in "Puyallup I," the landmark case *United States v. Washington* was under consideration in federal court in Tacoma. The case asked the federal court to protect the Tribes' fishing rights on all species in all of their usual and accustomed fishing places... with the exception of Puyallup River steelhead, which was the subject of *Washington State Department of Game v. Puyallup Tribe* in the state courts.

The plaintiffs were the federal government and 14 treaty tribes, including the Puyallup Tribe. That total increased to 21 over time as the complicated case worked its way through the courts. The defendants were the State of Washington and several state agencies and officials.

The federal government filed the case in an effort to protect the tribes' treaty rights and the tribal peoples themselves from the state-sanctioned violence that continued against the Indians and their families. The parties spent three years preparing for the case. The United States and the tribes compiled written reports about the tribes' history and culture, and the important role fishing played. They spelled out the importance of salmon and steelhead to the Indians' culture and religion and to their diet. The trial lasted for nearly four weeks and had almost 50 witnesses, including members of many tribes and expert witnesses. The transcripts were about 4,600 pages, with about 350 exhibits.

The tribes and their attorneys originally were not optimistic about *U.S. v. Washington* because it was assigned to Judge

George H. Boldt. He had been appointed by a Republican president and had a reputation for being extremely conservative. Judge Boldt, however, did his homework and gave all parties every opportunity to make all of the arguments they wished on every possible issue related to treaty fishing rights.

Judge Boldt was extremely impressed by the case put on by the United States and the tribes. When he made his decision and issued an opinion after four years of preparation, then trial, in the case, he commented on how impressed he was by the tribal elders and other witnesses who testified and by the anthropologist Dr. Barbara Lane, who testified for the U.S. and the tribes.

While Judge Boldt considered the issues in *United States v. Washington*, the Puyallup Tribe celebrated another victory in *Washington State Department of Game v. Puyallup Tribe*. Following "Puyallup I," the Court sent the case back to the state courts to determine whether prohibiting nets when tribal members fish for steelhead was reasonable and necessary for conservation. In the second round of the case, the Washington Supreme Court ruled that because the sport fishery took virtually all of the harvestable steelhead, banning net fishing by tribal members was necessary to conserve the species.

The Tribe appealed, and in a ruling known as "Puyallup II," the U.S. Supreme Court in 1973 reversed that ruling. It held that restricting all the steelhead for the sport fishery discriminated against the Tribe and therefore violated the treaty right. The Court ruled that the opportunity to catch steelhead must be divided between the sport fishery and tribal members, and sent the case back to the state courts to make that determination.

A year later, Judge Boldt released a groundbreaking decision in *Washington State Department of Game v. Puyallup Tribe*. He called his ruling in February, 1974 "Final Decision #1." In an extensive and detailed opinion, he held that the treaty tribes had a right to take 50% of the harvestable salmon in each run and a right to be co-managers of the fishery resource along with the State of Washington.

While the ruling provided reason for the Puyallup Indians to celebrate a personal and political victory, it carried with it a bittersweet note for the people who once enjoyed complete freedom to fish without answering to authorities and without seeing half of their catch confiscated. In addition, Judge Boldt's ruling set off a furor in western Washington. Newspaper articles and editorials, commercial and sport fishing organizations, and anti-Indian organizations of all types howled for Judge Boldt's impeachment and reversal of his ruling. The Washington Departments of Fisheries and Game refused to enforce the restrictions on non-treaty fisheries that were necessary to protect the tribes' opportunity. Ugly confrontations took place on rivers and in Puget Sound involving treaty and non-treaty fishers and state enforcement officers. Judge Boldt ordered state officials to protect the tribes' opportunity to fish; the Washington Supreme Court told state officials they couldn't do that. Chaos reigned.

U.S. v. Washington on appeal

Judge Boldt's ruling and the Tribe's fishing rights were confirmed and vindicated when the decision was appealed. The Ninth Circuit Court of Appeals upheld "Final Decision #1" in 1975, sending a loud, clear message to the Tribe's opponents that Judge Boldt's ruling was correct and was not some wild and crazy departure from the law. The U.S. Supreme Court in 1976 refused to review the case.

Those appeals should have brought an end to the controversy over the Tribe's treaty fishing rights. Unfortunately, however, the State, the non-treaty fishing groups, and the media were not about to give up their fight. When state officials and courts refused to enforce what the federal courts had said was the law, the tribes' right to an opportunity to fish continued to be trampled.

The tribes ramped up their fight, both on the water and in the courts. One thing working in their favor was that federal judges do not look kindly on parties that violate federal court orders. When the State's fishing agencies refused to enforce restrictions on the non-Indian (non-treaty) commercial fishing groups, Judge Boldt in 1977 issued an injunction directly against those groups and ordered U.S. Marshals to enforce the injunction.

The ruling was even more controversial than "Final Decision #1" because the fishing groups (like the purse seiners and the gillnetters) were not parties to *U.S. v. Washington*. Those groups, loudly supported by the media, yelled and screamed that Judge Boldt could not touch them. They appealed the injunction. The Ninth Circuit Court of Appeals was highly critical of the State's and the fishing groups' violations of Judge Boldt's order:

> "The state's extraordinary machinations in resisting the decree have forced the district court [Judge Boldt] to take over a large share of the management of the state's fishery in order to enforce its decrees. Except for some desegregation cases..., the district court has faced the most concerted official and private efforts to frustrate a decree of a federal court witnessed in this century."

Because of the fishing groups' complete refusal to respect the tribes' treaty fishing rights, and because the fishing groups were very well aware of the requirements of Judge Boldt's orders, the

Court of Appeals in 1977 upheld the injunction and ruled that the federal court could enforce it against the groups.

Puyallup III

Amidst the controversy and the federal courts' rulings, *Washington State Department of Game v. Puyallup Tribe* continued its third round in Washington state courts. The Pierce County Superior Court took up the U.S. Supreme Court's assignment to divide the Puyallup River steelhead between the sport fishery and tribal members. Judge Boldt had ruled that the treaty language "in common with all citizens of the Territory" meant that each side is entitled to 50% of the harvestable fish in each run. In what the Tribe viewed as sour grapes and a cheap shot at the Tribe, the Superior Court ruled for no particular reason that tribal members were entitled to only 45% of the harvestable steelhead. Even more damaging, the Superior Court ruled that this right applied only to native steelhead and not to the much larger number of hatchery-raised steelhead.

The Washington Supreme Court upheld the Superior Court's decision, and the case went for the third time to the U.S. Supreme Court. The opinion in "Puyallup III" in 1977 has become a landmark one not for its rulings on fishing issues but because of its confirmation, at long last, that the Puyallup Tribe's sovereign immunity prevents the state courts from exercising jurisdiction over the Tribe. The decision has become one of the benchmark rulings on tribal sovereign immunity. The case is regularly cited for that principle even though the rulings in "Puyallup III" on fishing issues have faded to obscurity. Before we explore the fate of that case, however, we switch back to a central chapter of *U.S. v. Washington*.

U.S. v. Washington in the U.S. Supreme Court

The fishing groups appealed Judge Boldt's injunction to the U.S. Supreme Court. After refusing to review "Final Decision #1" in the case, the court agreed to review the entire case when the fishing groups appealed the Ninth Circuit's ruling on the injunction. Although the winning side in a case—the United States and the tribes in this case—usually don't want to see a case appealed further, the tribes realized that the only way to quiet the controversy over Judge Boldt's rulings was probably to have a U.S. Supreme Court ruling on the case.

That came about in 1979. The justices ruled 6–3 to uphold both "Final Decision #1" and Judge Boldt's injunction against the fishing groups. The Supreme Court ruled that the treaty fishing rights indeed included the tribes' right to take 50% of the harvestable salmon, at least when that was necessary in order to earn a "moderate livelihood."

Although there continued to be sporadic attempts to undermine *U.S. v. Washington*, the Supreme Court's ruling went a long way toward institutionalizing the decision and the tribes' fishing rights. The striking change in the attitude of the state's fisheries managers is a lasting legacy of the case.

Department of Game v. Puyallup Tribe concludes

After the Supreme Court sent "Puyallup III" back to the state courts in 1977, Pierce County Superior Court continued to interfere with the Tribe's fishing rights for a few years longer. Despite the Tribe's immunity from suit, the Supreme Court in "Puyallup III" had upheld the authority of the state courts to enforce conservation restrictions on the fishing activities of tribal members. An overly zealous Superior Court judge took up that invitation. He ruled, for example, that tribal members could not participate in the steelhead harvest unless they first provided the court with copies of their income tax returns; he based that requirement on the "moderate livelihood" language in the Supreme Court's review of *U.S. v. Washington*. Tribal members refused to do that. For a couple of years they were, therefore, not permitted to fish for steelhead.

After 17 long years, however, the Tribe finally succeeded in bringing the case to an end. It made no sense to have one case in the state courts affecting one run of fish on one river when the federal court in *U.S. v. Washington* was making rulings on every other run of fish in western Washington using a different set of standards than those used by the state courts. The Pierce County Superior Court judge finally agreed. In 1980 he granted the Tribe's motion to dismiss the case on the condition that the federal court in *U.S. v. Washington* would include Puyallup River steelhead in the rulings it made. From that point forward, all runs of fish on all rivers have been managed and harvested under the same set of legal standards.

U.S. v. Washington, other major treaty fishing rights issues

U.S. v. Washington has had an active case under the continuing jurisdiction of the federal district court ever since it was originally filed. During the nearly 40 years of the case, the court has dealt with a number of other important issues that are part of the tribes' treaty fishing rights.

Hatchery fish

The federal court disagreed with the state courts' ruling in "Puyallup III" that the treaty right applies only to native fish. In *U.S. v. Washington* the federal court ruled that hatchery fish are included under the treaty right. The Ninth Circuit upheld that ruling, and the U.S. Supreme Court refused to disturb it. That ruling is vital to the tribes' fishing rights. The majority of fish in most of the runs are hatchery fish. If they were not included in the treaty right, there would not be enough fish to make fishing practical for tribal members. That would be particularly unjust because tribes raise a major share of the hatchery fish and release them for everyone to harvest.

Shellfish

A later part of *U.S. v. Washington* ruled that the legal principles governing management and harvest of salmon apply as well to shellfish. As a result, the state, and the court are heavily involved in the management of that resource, including geoduck, clams, oysters, prawns, and shrimp. The Puyallup Tribe's shellfish department licenses tribal members for that harvest, sets safety standards for the very dangerous activities involved, and works with other tribes and the state to manage those resources.

Protection of the fishery habitat

As a result of *U.S. v. Washington*, tribal governments have had an opportunity to develop their own fisheries' management programs. The Puyallup Tribe's Fisheries Division is a shining example. The department manages the fishery harvest by tribal members, supplements the fishery resource with fish raised in the Tribe's fish hatcheries, and works to protect and restore the fishery habitat. The Puyallup Tribe's Fisheries Division serves to protect, preserve, and enhance the five species of the Pacific salmon in the Tribe's usual and accustomed areas, and the water resources that determine their viability. Working in tandem with other tribal departments and cooperating with numerous county, state, and federal agencies, the Puyallup Tribe's fisheries department produces annual spawning reports for Puyallup River Watershed salmon, steelhead, and char and continually monitors salmon runs in the Puyallup River.

The legal battle over protection of the fishery habitat has been extended. The principle is extremely important because without protection and restoration of the habitat, the decades-long decline in the number of fish will continue. That hurts the fisheries of Indians and non-Indians alike.

In 1980, the federal district court ruled (again as part of *U.S. v. Washington*) that the tribes' treaty right includes the right to have the habitat protected from harm. The Ninth Circuit upheld part of that ruling but cut back on other parts. In 1982, the Ninth Circuit reconsidered and vacated the ruling, sending the issue back to the district court and instructing the parties to bring to the court a specific habitat-related situation for the litigation.

The issue sat still for about 15 years. In 2001, the U.S. government and the tribes filed a proceeding involving a more specific example: harm caused to the fishery resource and habitat by culverts blocking fish passage in streams. In 2007, the district court ruled that those culverts violate the treaty by harming the fishery resource and decreasing the number of salmon available for all fisheries. The district court is currently considering what the state should be ordered to do to fix that problem.

Usual and accustomed fishing grounds

Once the courts had affirmed the tribes' treaty fishing rights and the state had finally begun enforcing restrictions on the non-treaty fishery, some of the tribes' focus in the case went in another direction. There have unfortunately been a number of disputes between and among tribes over the extent of each tribe's usual and accustomed fishing grounds. Those have been vigorously litigated in the federal district court and court of appeals in *U.S. v. Washington*.

The Puyallup Tribe has protected its access to its fishing

grounds by reaching agreements with other tribes concerning the Tribe's usual and accustomed fishing grounds. The Puyallup, Nisqually, and Squaxin Island tribes reached an agreement spelling out the three tribes' respective fishing areas in the South Sound. An agreement with the Tulalip tribes concerning Tulalip's fishing grounds provides some protection for fish heading back to the Puyallup River when those fish pass through the waters of northern Puget Sound.

Conclusion

U.S. v. Washington has been in the federal court for 40 years and continues forward. It is one of the most remarkable cases in American history in any subject area, and a landmark among Indian tribes' struggles and battles to protect their rights against both the intentional and inadvertent attacks by the larger society.

CHAPTER 7

CASCADIA TAKEOVER

When the Tacoma Indian Hospital opened with fanfare in the early 1940s, it was praised not only as a modern, state-of-the-art facility, but as a symbol of Northwest Native American resilience and determination. The hospital emblemized the government keeping its agreements concerning a key provision of the Medicine Creek Treaty, namely that of government provided education and health care for all tribal members. Local officials involved in the project swelled with pride over the facility (and what they had "done for the Indians"), and headlines in the *Tacoma News Tribune* declared, "Indian Treaty Kept" and "No other hospital like it."

The grounds on which the hospital was built, more commonly known as Cushman, are sacred to the Puyallup Tribe. The area is known to Indians throughout the country. The land had been occupied and visited by thousands of Indian people reaching back centuries before the white man came. Several

Part of the takeover of Cascadia included positioning armed Tribal guards on the rooftops to keep watch and help keep everyone safe inside. Courtesy of Andy De Los Angeles Collection.

villages once stood within close proximity, making it a popular gathering site. It was a favorite place to hold Indian bone games, potlatches, ball games, salmon bakes, powwows, funerals, and meetings for social and religious purposes. It was a regular stopping place for many headed into the valley for summertime work such as picking hops and berries.

Portions of the acreage include the old Puyallup graveyard containing an unknown number of burials. During construction of a road for the reservation school in 1902, the skeleton of a Puyallup Indian was discovered on the western end of the school grounds, covered by two feet of soil beneath a tree that was estimated to be 200 years old. Efforts to preserve the burial ground against the encroachment of civilization were difficult, but the Tribe retained enough of the land to continue the use of the Cushman Indian Cemetery.

The Cushman property went through many changes over the years following the white man's arrival, but it always remained a site for education and health care facilities for the Puyallup Tribe and other Indians in the region. The Tacoma Indian Hospital, also called Cushman Hospital, finally offered tribal members a variety of medical services, a most welcome improvement over what had been offered so far in the way of health care. However, in keeping with past patterns of governmental sleight-of-hand in its dealings with Native populations, it wouldn't be long before the government would attempt to take the hospital away behind the backs of the very people it was built for and on whose land the hospital stood according to the internationally recognized Medicine Creek Treaty.

Costing about $1.5 million to construct, a big price tag in those years, the sprawling hospital was a broad and imposing six-story structure on a 38-acre site overlooking Tacoma from

Tacoma Indian Hospital received many Alaskan tribal patients who were taken to the hospital to receive treatment for TB, 1956. Courtesy Ione Knox Collection.

its eastern city limits on East 28th Street. Built of sturdy brick, steel, and concrete to resist fires and last for decades, the 350-bed hospital housed patients from enrolled members of federally recognized tribes in Washington, Oregon, Idaho, Montana, Alaska and northern California. Attracting Indian patients from across the country as well, the hospital was also known as the U.S. Indian Hospital because it served any enrolled tribal member from coast to coast who walked through the door.

In the early 1950s a renewed wave of tuberculosis (TB) hit hard among Northwest tribal communities. Many tribal members suffered great pain, and even more died, including children and elders. In 1955 the Cushman Hospital was converted from a general hospital into a TB sanatorium. The administration was also switched at this time from the Department of Interior's Bureau of Indian Affairs (BIA) to the Department of Health, Education and Welfare (HEW) of the U.S. Public Health Service. Tribal members employed at the hospital lost their jobs due to the shift in care provided, and responsibility for furnishing general medicinal care to the local Indian population was transferred to local agencies.

Over the next few years, incidents of TB among the tribes dropped off. Word began to spread that the hospital would possibly close after the Washington State Dept. of Institutions expressed an interest in acquiring the land and facility to use as a diagnostics center for juvenile offenders. The decision to close the hospital rested with the HEW, and its fate didn't hang in the balance for long. For five years the Tribe worked to get the Cushman site back to establish the Chief Leschi Indian Medical Building, but to no avail. Despite the Tribe's best efforts to save their hospital, HEW ruled that the hospital had outlived its purpose and declared it surplus to Indian health needs. HEW

Ramona Bennett (second from left) and other supporters of the Cascadia takeover argue for their tribal demands during one of many marathon negotiating sessions with state and federal officials (the two white men in suits). Pictured also are Puyallup tribal members Alison Bridges (seated on floor next to Bennett), her mother Maiselle Bridges (leaning forward in front of table lamp) and Edith McCloud (to Maiselle's left in front of painting). Courtesy of the Freedom Socialist.

announced in 1959 it would close the hospital for good.

Adding insult to injury for the Tribe, the government handed ownership over to the state with no voice or involvement from the owners, the Puyallups. A deed was executed July 10, 1961, for the term of 20 years. With the closure of Cushman Hospital, Washington, Oregon, and Idaho made up the only Indian Health Service region in the country without a hospital. Now the state had in its hands the multi-million dollar property and building complex while the Puyallups were virtually ignored. They didn't take it lying down.

Upon the closure of Cushman, the Puyallup Tribe said the property should revert to them since the federal government had failed to maintain an Indian hospital on the grounds, in keeping with signed agreements made in 1939 when the Tribe deeded the land to the government for that specific purpose. Members of the Tribe were angry at the government's audacity to dispose of their hospital and hand it over to the state. Moreover, doing so was a flagrant disregard of treaty provisions. Like a game of keep-away between the feds and state, quality medical care for the Tribe was given, then taken away, many times over during the Tribe's dealings with the federal government.

A committee formed among local tribal leaders and activists, charged with drafting a constitution and by-laws for the reactivation of the Northwest Federation of American Indians. Originally organized in Tacoma in 1914 and consisting of representative leaders from most of the dominant Indian tribes in the Northwest, the federation had the power to negotiate treaties and contracts with the federal government.

Northwest tribal communities mobilized and staged several gatherings of important players including the Conference of Northwest Indians on March 14, 1959. A reported 150 tribal members from Minnesota to Oklahoma and throughout the West filled the hospital auditorium with Tacoma civic leaders, attorneys, doctors, and other friends of the Tribe. Their intention was to alert Congress to the issue and convince political leaders in the nation's capitol to reverse HEW's decision. They wanted to bring Cushman back as a general hospital and social service center serving Indians, with a separate ward for treating TB. Even though TB rates had declined, Indian people were still afflicted by serious illnesses stemming from poverty and poor diet as a result of government neglect. Support for the Tribe to keep the hospital came from many fronts, particularly the United Presbyterian Church Synod of Washington, which had been operating the Tacoma Indian Mission on the hospital grounds.

It soon became clear that the government had no true interest in taking the tribes' demands seriously, and upon recommendation by the Washington State Council for Children and Youth the state officially took possession of the hospital in 1961 to make way for a juvenile diagnostic and treatment center with facilities for 235 boys and 30–35 girls. The state legislature approved approximately $1.5 million for remodeling and operations costs.

For nearly 20 years beginning around 1963, the Cascadia Juvenile Reception and Diagnostic Center ran what amounted to a jail where delinquent youngsters 13–18 were "observed" and dealt with in a number of ways. Reports of squalid conditions and abuse of the children plagued the center throughout its existence. It grew particularly notorious among tribal members, some of whom knew what it was like there from their own children and that of their friends'. Those on the outside heard stories repeatedly of inhuman conditions in a prison-like environment,

The Cascadia takeover served as a rallying point for many political activists at the time, who used the occasion to bring attention to the suffering of Indians everywhere. Courtesy of the Freedom Socialist.

Sign of the times. Courtesy of the Freedom Socialist.

with its unheated, windowless cells that buzzed with mosquitoes and stank of filth.

The state stood fast in its refusal to return the Cascadia property to the Puyallup people, who never gave up the fight to reclaim their property legally. In the summer of 1973, tribal members erected two teepees on the Cascadia grounds as visual symbols of Indian presence.

A key roadblock was set up by then-Governor Dan Evans. When approached by the Puyallup Tribal Council to give the land back in keeping with the federal treaty, Evans said he would do so provided the state would be reimbursed the $1.5 million in remodeling and operations costs it had already put into the place.

Taking the governor at his word, a delegation of Puyallup Tribal Council members and representatives of other area tribes traveled to Washington, D.C. to meet with anyone who would be willing to listen and help the Tribe secure the reimbursement funds. During their trip, Gov. Evans opened a Pandora's Box when he informed Tribal Council Chair Ramona Bennett that he didn't plan to give up Cascadia even if the Tribe did come up with the reimbursement money. A sense of righteous outrage swept through the membership at the governor's broken promise. Tribal leadership knew it was time to seize the day.

Once the delegation returned from the nation's capitol, the Tribal Council announced that a powwow would be held in the medical services clinic that had been established for tribal members on the fifth floor of the Cascadia complex. On October 23, 1976, drums played in celebration of this modest clinic, and about 200 members of the Puyallup Tribe and their friends stood shoulder to shoulder. It would be an evening to remember. This eyewitness account from Seattle journalist Sam Deaderick explains why:

"At approximately 6:15 p.m., after 150 juvenile prisoners incarcerated in detention units finished dinner, a band of 50 Indians descended from their 5th floor open house and casually swarmed through the huge main building. Accompanied by their tribal police, who are always uniformed and armed while on duty, they firmly served a previously prepared eviction notice on the assistant shift officer, then seized the switchboard and assumed control of the building. In the calm but decisive act of revolutionary transformation of property relations, they completed the expropriation by announcing that the entire institution was, in the words of...the Puyallup Tribal Council, 'in the possession of the Puyallup Tribe of Indians as its sovereign and rightful owners.'"

The takeover shocked not only the state; it seemed as if the entire Northwest was holding its collective breath for the next seven days while the Tribe and supporters occupied the building and handled all administrative duties, including serving three meals a day to up to 200 people. Tribal fishermen brought in their catch, and supporters hauled in boxes of groceries and other donations. A complex security system was set in place complete with sentries at the entry gate and on the rooftops. Binoculars and walkie-talkies were handed out to those in charge. The Indian clinic remained open, childcare was organized, and friendly visitors were welcome. The juvenile residents were tended to with care.

During the occupation, spirits remained high as money and telegrams continually came in from supporters. Tribal members from across Indian country came to join the insurrection, as did people of all races including African-Americans, whites, and Latinos. Hundreds of telegrams were sent to government officials demanding the Tribe receive what was rightfully theirs. Reporters and photographers swarmed the place awaiting a newsbreak, and press conferences were held at which speakers called on governmental leaders to avoid violence against the Indians and negotiate in good faith. Finally the Puyallup Tribe had the world's attention on this most critical matter.

Deaderick described it like this: "Throughout the day the building echoed with the triumphant high-pitched chant of the American Indian Movement (AIM) anthem resounding against the throbbing beat of a large drum decorated with the symbol of the 'Trail of Self-determination.' People worked tirelessly, and behind the apparent chaos an atmosphere of order, dignity, and humor prevailed. The mood was one of watchful high spirits. Federal marshals and troops with overkill firepower could arrive at any moment and everyone knew it, yet the entire occupation force was prepared to stay through to the end."

The Cascadia takeover never turned violent, although armed tribal guards were ready to mobilize should law enforcement have tried to forcibly remove them. The Puyallup Tribe proved to be not only determined, but smart in how they orchestrated the delicate situation—from the gentle and compassionate manner in which the youthful Cascadia inmates were handled, to the takeover leaders' open readiness to talk with state and federal authorities to solve the dispute through diplomacy. No one wanted another Wounded Knee, even though heavily armed U.S. Marshals stood by ready for the order to swarm the place.

Representatives from the state and U.S. governments traveled to the Puyallup reservation to take part in the talks. A key player in the negotiations was Undersecretary of the Dept. of Interior R. Dennis Ickes, who said his intention was to help the Puyallups get their property back to be held in trust by the U.S.

As the days passed during the Cascadia occupation, more and more supporters arrived to lend support and take part in spontaneous prayers, songs and other rallying actions. Courtesy of the Freedom Socialist.

government. This was the Puyallups' intention as well, which made for a mutually agreeable starting point although on a rocky road.

Negotiations with Ickes and state officials from the Department of Social and Health Services (DSHS) seemed to be making progress, but the state moved to seek an injunction against the Tribe in federal court to bar the Puyallups from occupying Cascadia. A restraining order enforceable by federal marshals was issued and stood poised to be enacted if negotiations weren't met by a court-ordered deadline.

Minutes before the clock struck the hour to remove the tribal occupants, a two-part agreement was reached: 1.) In return for the Puyallups and their supporters vacating the premises, one building and about eight acres of land would immediately revert to government ownership for tribal use, and 2.) the Secretary of the Department of the Interior would review the state's claim to the facility and, depending on the findings, would "take immediate and appropriate action…for the return of the total property to the trusteeship of the United States for the Tribe."

Finally the Tribe was not only heard, but state and federal promises were made before the public and sealed in writing. The Cascadia takeover had won the Tribe much publicity, and now the public eye was focused on the situation with anticipation for a peaceful outcome. Tribal members vacated the buildings, bursting into song and celebration dances on the front lawns. The state agreed to file no criminal charges against those involved in the armed takeover. The Tribe didn't declare total victory, but saw that there had been giant steps to winning a battle for their sacred lands that had lasted for so many years. As everyone vacated the building, Tribal Council Chair Bennett, who took the lead in the takeover from the beginning, spoke into

Chanting their demands, Cascadia occupants raise their fists defiantly. Courtesy of the Freedom Socialist.

It was necessary for those occupying the Cascadia building to be on guard night and day, including making rounds in makeshift patrol cars. Courtesy of the Freedom Socialist.

After seizing the building, activists unfurled a banner to rename the facility Chief Leschi Indian Medical Building (C.L.I.M.B.). Courtesy of the Freedom Socialist.

a bullhorn amid thunderous applause and cheers. "The next time we come in we'll have the deed, and we'll hold a real big open house. And we won't have to worry about any federal marshals coming in and blowing down the building."

Cascadia Juvenile Diagnostic Center went back into scaled-down operation following the takeover, and with fewer young people than before within its cells. Juvenile offenders were being diverted to other state institutions until the courts decided who owned Cascadia. Meanwhile, the Tribe never let up in its quest to evict the state from their property. The question remained as to the validity of the deed that transferred the property from the federal government to the state, and the state continued to request reimbursement for the capital improvements it invested in the site.

The issue remained in the courts for the next several years, and was brought to a head in 1980 following a separate U.S. Supreme Court ruling that struck a blow to the tribal economy. The court issued a decision to uphold state taxation of Indian smoke shop cigarette sales to non-Indians, a decision that would negatively impact sales at reservation smoke shops. This amounted to another strike against the Puyallup Indians, whose economy depended heavily on revenue from tobacco purchases at the many smoke shops around the reservation.

To bring attention to this latest ruling against them, the Tribe punctuated its stand on June 12, 1980, when tribal police blockaded all entrances to the Cascadia Juvenile Diagnostic Center. The state should pay rent to the Tribe to do business on their reservation, the Puyallups asserted, an idea supported throughout the membership as a way to offset revenue the Tribe faced losing from reduced cigarette sales. The blockade brought additional focus on the struggle for Cascadia as well, and pressured the courts to make a decision.

The Puyallups ultimately prevailed. A week later, U.S. District Court Judge Jack Tanner ruled that the state did not belong on the Cushman property. The center belonged to the federal government to be held in trust for the Puyallup Tribe, Tanner ruled, and the transfer of the property to the state was "null and void." By December of that same year, many of the Tribe's programs had moved into the building and the name Cascadia faded away as the Tribal Administration Building took root. The tribal law enforcement division was one of the first to set up offices there along with the tribal Planning and Land Use Department, and Chief Leschi School held classes for middle and high school students in the early 1980s.

Over the ensuing years, the nearly 50-year-old building began to show signs of wear and need of serious upgrades. In October of 1991, several engineering and architecture firms reported deficiencies in the structure, finding it so unstable that it could be severely damaged by a windstorm or collapse in an earthquake. With the building frame so shaky, asbestos and lead paint to deal with, and contaminants present from underground hospital waste, inspections determined it would be cost-prohibitive to remodel the Administration Building that had already weathered so many social and political storms. The building was torn down in 2003 and the land was put to use as overflow parking for the Emerald Queen Casino, and today it is the site of the Puyallup Tribe's new 26,000-square-foot Elders Center, a $13 million project that serves as an exemplary model of tribal respect and care for elders.

Puyallup activists parked vans bumper-to-bumper to block the entry to Cascadia Juvenile Reception and Diagnostic Center. Courtesy of the Freedom Socialist.

Tribal members erected teepees on the Cascadia grounds as symbols of Indian presence. Courtesy of the Freedom Socialist.

CHAPTER 8

TRIBAL LAW ENFORCEMENT

Following the Boldt decision in 1974, the Puyallup Tribe had the right to 50 percent of the fishing in the area, but no way to protect those rights. Non-Native fishers and fishing organizations protested the decision, and sometimes would defy it and fish anyway. While the Puyallup Tribe had its own security force and a way of addressing disputes among tribal members, it had no way of stopping others from breaking laws or violating rights.

The Puyallup Tribal Police Department—established and recognized by the Bureau of Indian Affairs (BIA) in 1975—was established with the primary responsibility of protecting the Tribe's fishing rights. In its earliest years the department was housed in a tribal fisheries building on Pioneer and River roads. There were five officers—three for patrolling the land, and two for patrolling the water. The department had a tiny budget. Its only vehicle was a Jeep Cherokee, called the Golden Eagle, which was used primarily for fisheries enforcement.

The first years of the department were dominated by the assertion and protection of the Tribe's rights. In its first year of existence, department officers assisted in the two-week non-violent takeover of Cascadia Juvenile Diagnostic Center, which the Tribe asserted was illegally transferred from the BIA to the state. The police department's primary role in the standoff was to make sure it remained non-violent.

During the first few years, the police department was hindered by its inability to detain those who violated the law. Because the department had no incarceration facilities, officers only had the ability to cite offenders and release them. For serious crimes, officers would do an initial investigation and arrest, then turn over the case to the BIA for further investigation. The department worked with the Department of Fish and Wildlife to conduct patrols of the Puyallup River for illegal activity. The department was also responsible for safeguarding the tribal community and membership, and for patrolling the administration building. By 1979 the department had nearly 10 officers plus a chief of police and two lieutenants, and two or three vehicles.

In the mid-1970s the police department relocated to the old tribal administration building, on top of the hill near the tribal cemetery. The department relocated again, in the late 1970s, to a mobile home on 32nd and Grandview streets. The department moved for a third time to a house near where the Interstate 5 casino now stands. Also during the late 1970s, the Tribe helped operate the Kwatee group home, a safe place for at-risk children to stay. The home operated until 1982.

The 1980s saw significant changes and growth in the police department. Following the second Cascadia takeover in 1980, the police department relocated to the basement of the building, where it remained into the early 1990s. The department included jail cells—six for men, called the "Deep Six," and two dormitories for woman.

Within a few years of the establishment of the tribal police department, the Tribe was able to assert its fishing rights; fisheries enforcement, while still important, no longer dominated the department's time. During the 1980s, individual Tribal members operated two nightclubs, at which Tribal officers responded to such incidents as bar fights. Four Tribal bingo halls also generated calls to the police department, mostly for cheating on pull-tabs, and also occasionally for vehicle theft and vandalism.

In 1982 a new police chief joined the department and began to stress training, sending his officers to both state and BIA instruction. This training made officers more confident and better able to serve the community. The department fluctuated in size during this decade due to budget constraints. The department's inability to pay competitive wages meant that the Tribe often lost recruits to other departments. At one time during the 1980s the Tribe had only four officers.

Also in the 1980s, the police department started to have a presence in Chief Leschi Schools. The department assigned a resource officer to the schools and also operated programs like DARE, to help students combat the temptations of drugs. At the same time, gang issues slowly began to arise in low-income areas of the reservation. Hunting issues also became a priority for law enforcement. The Tribe began to establish its own regulations as the police department grew.

Through the 1980s, the Tribe had no authority to arrest non-Natives, even on reservation property. The U.S. Supreme Court, in its decision in the case of *Oliphant v. Suquamish Indian Tribe*,

Puyallup Tribal police force patrols the reservation and beyond, such as at the Puyallup Fair.

determined that tribal courts do not have inherent criminal jurisdiction, and therefore cannot try or punish non-Natives unless specifically authorized to do so by Congress. The decision came in 1978, just three years after the establishment of the Puyallup Tribal Police Department.

In the late 1980s, relationships with other law enforcement and government agencies began to develop. These relationships were pivotal in the development of the Land Claims Settlement of 1988, which had a big impact on the Tribal police department. Following the settlement, all the governments involved got together to discuss how to best serve their communities. In 1991, a cross commission, consisting of the Tacoma, Pierce County, and Fife police departments, the state patrol, the FBI and the BIA, came together to address jurisdictional issues. The cross-commission helped to fill law enforcement gaps.

From that commission came important agreements with the Tacoma Police Department and the Pierce County Sheriff's Department, which allowed tribal police to arrest non-Natives on the reservation and book them into the appropriate state or municipal jail, depending on the charges. Natives would still be booked into the Puyallup Tribal jail unless a warrant existed with another jurisdiction. A similar agreement, allowing tribal police to arrest non-Natives on trust property, was signed with the city of Fife in 2004. The Puyallup Tribal Police Department has also discussed implementing a similar agreement with the city of Puyallup. The agreements also give the tribal police the ability to give citations to anyone within reservation boundaries.

The Land Claims Settlement ushered in a new era of cooperation between the Puyallup Tribe's police department and other governmental agencies. While previously many jurisdictions had dismissed the tribal police as undertrained, following the settlement they came to realize that tribal officers were highly trained and professional. The Tribal police began working with other agencies to address such issues as the increasing gang problems on and near the reservation, which continued to grow into the 1990s. The new era of cooperation has helped the Tribe deal effectively with many of the gang problems that have plagued the area. The Tribe also became more involved in emergency preparedness, particularly for such threats to the tribal community as flooding and earthquakes.

After spending more than a decade in the basement of the Cascadia building, the BIA declared the facility unsafe. The department moved again to a building in the current I-5 casino parking lot. The department moved again to the old Chief Leschi elementary school when a new one was constructed before moving to its current location.

Another jail, established in the late 1980s or early 1990s, was established at the end of East 29th Street. The facility included five dormitory-style lock-downs. It was damaged during the 2001 Nisqually earthquake and the Tribe discontinued use of the facility, instead using a doublewide trailer as a temporary solution. The trailer has two cells, each with an occupancy of five or six inmates. The police department also has contracts with the Nisqually and Chehalis police departments for use of their jails, and with Remann Hall, where the Tribal police send juvenile inmates.

The Emerald Queen Casinos also brought new challenges—and new opportunities—to the Tribal police department. With their construction, the Tribal police department shifted much of its attention to maintaining law and order at the casino locations. Officers began responding to calls about stolen cars, vandal-

A scene from a general membership meeting of the Puyallup Tribe in the 1970s. From left: Marie Henry, secretary; Frank Wright, Sr.; Don Matheson; Alison Bridges; and tribal attorney John Bell. Courtesy of the Puyallup Tribe.

ism, prostitution, fraudulent checks, and cheating. At the same time, the casinos brought a lot of money to the Tribe, much of which was diverted to law enforcement, allowing the department to fund more officers, better equipment, and more training. Whereas during the 1980s and 1990s the Tribe depended on the BIA for much of its funding, the casinos allowed the Tribe to begin to fund more of its law enforcement activities. The Tribe was able to develop a more specialized police department and helped the Tribe's law enforcement become what it is today.

Much of the growth over the last decade can be attributed to the casinos. In the last 10 years, the Tribe's law enforcement staff has nearly doubled. Calls for service have greatly increased, but with it, so has funding from the tribal council, grants and other entities. Today, the tribal police department has a full staff of 30 sworn officers and nine civilian employees who are in charge of dispatch and corrections.

At the top of the police department is the chief of police. Four patrol lieutenants handle 12-hour shifts, each with four or five officers. They respond to day-to-day calls for service. One investigation lieutenant is responsible for the department's two full-time detectives, who handle investigations, as well as two narcotics detectives, the school resource officer at Chief Leschi School, and the Tribe's housing officers. Puyallup Tribal police officers go through the same state training as other officers. They receive tribal certification from the state when the mandatory training is completed. The corrections supervisor oversees eight correction workers, who also serve as dispatchers.

Thanks to the increased cooperation among jurisdictions and police departments in recent years, the Puyallup Tribal Police Department has been able to partner on many different projects. The Tribe has several officers who have specialized training in gang response. The officers work with other Pierce County jurisdictions on a regional task force to have larger emphasis patrols both on the reservation and elsewhere in the county. The Tribe also has three officers assigned to the Pierce County Metro Lab team, which targets and shuts down methamphetamine labs in the area.

The Puyallups also work with other tribal police departments. The Tribe has partnered with the Lummi, Tulalip, Swinomish, and Stillaguamish tribes to share resources and officers for undercover investigations, large tribal events and other operations. The partnership recently began after two years in development.

The Puyallup Tribe also partners with other jurisdictions to train and respond to such events as flooding and other emergency situations.

Fisheries enforcement remains vitally important to the Tribe and the livelihood of many Puyallups. The Tribal police have four boats and two jet skis, and all officers receive specialized training in how to handle boats. Enforcement of fishing regulations remains difficult, as officers have a large area to enforce. More recently, the police department has begun to enforce crabbing, shrimping, and geoduck and shellfish harvesting regulations. About half of the police department's resources are dedicated to fisheries, and even more during fishing and shellfish seasons.

The Tribal police department also faces challenges in the form of gangs and drug problems. These challenges have prompted the department to dedicate two detectives to narcotics enforcement. A school resource officer works to effect positive changes at Chief Leschi School. The Gang Resistance Education and Training (GREAT) program includes summer classes and short weekend camps, and helps to address gang problems and drug issues among the Tribe's youth.

About six years ago, the Tribe's law enforcement department began working to address public safety on the reservation and in the larger area. A new Tribal public safety office works with the Pierce County Department of Emergency Management, the Federal Emergency Management Agency and other entities to prepare for manmade and natural disasters. The agencies work together mostly on prevention and emergency planning.

The public safety office also works within the Tribe. The office works with the police department to monitor conditions and to notify Tribal members to evacuate should an emergency necessitate it. The public safety office also works with the health department and Chief Leschi School to prepare for and respond to emergency situations.

More recently, the Puyallup Tribal Council also formed an emergency management committee to supplement and aid the work of the public safety office.

The Puyallup Tribal Police Department faces challenges going into the future. New challenges will arise as the casinos grow and other economic development increases—particularly at the Port of Tacoma. The role of the police department in law enforcement at the Tribe's terminals at the port remains unclear, but the Tribe could be facing new jurisdictional questions, as well as homeland security and emergency management responsibilities.

The Puyallup Tribe also has designed a new Criminal Justice Center, which would include all areas of law enforcement, including the police department, a 28-bed jail, public safety, probation and the Tribal court. The center has been designed, and is currently planned to be located just down the hill from the Elders Center in the I-5 casino parking lot.

The Tribal police department has progressed significantly in the more than 30 years it has been in operation. The department started with very little; over time and with the help of casinos, it has grown into a highly trained, professional organization. Partnerships with other police departments, both tribal and non-tribal, continue to flourish. The Tribe's police department plays a significant role not only among the Tribal community, but in the broader community, as the department aids with non-Native calls and operations both on and off the reservation. While the department has seen its share of ups and downs, service continues to improve. As the Tribe gets more resources, the police department becomes more highly trained and specialized. As the Tribe continues to grow, so too will the Tribal police department and court system.

CHAPTER 9

LAND CLAIMS SETTLEMENT OF 1988

The Puyallup Tribe's quest to have access to and control of its traditional lands is a long and complex story that begins with the Medicine Creek Treaty of 1854. Under the treaty the Tribe was allocated a reservation of 1,200 acres along Commencement Bay. In 1857 the reservation was expanded by a presidential executive order to 18,063.5 acres, the size it remains today. This is but a mere fraction of the lands on which the Puyallups once lived freely.

Despite their efforts to live in peace with the newcomers, Puyallups were relegated to reserved parcels of acreage from where they saw their homelands disappear as quickly as their familiar river banks, beaches, fishing grounds, gathering places, and wooded trails fell to the hands of homesteaders and commercial interests. The soil under the Puyallups' feet became, over time, valuable real estate that business and government entities eyed with interest and laid claim to without the Tribe's knowledge or consent.

But the Puyallup Tribe of Indians proved to be tenacious fighters in this and other battles. They did not walk away from their losses, but rather rallied to win back as much of their land as they could. A watershed event occurred in the 1980s with the great Land Claims Settlement of 1988.

The story begins prior to the 1980s. For years the Puyallup Tribal Council attempted to address legal issues that prevented them from receiving land that had mysteriously gone out of trust. Documents were collected through diligent research proving how the Tribe had been swindled out of much of their land, leaving many non-tribal members with the realization that they in fact did not hold clear title to their land holdings.

Two Tribal members who made critical contributions to the research—Frank Wright, Sr. and Silas Cross—traveled far and wide, from libraries in San Francisco to the Smithsonian in Washington, D.C. Later Frank Wright, Jr., Silas Cross' niece and tribal historian Judy Wright, and longtime tribal council member Bill Sterud continued this research with non-Indian historian Bob Waller and other experts and lawyers hired to assist the Tribe in getting justice for their land claims issues.

During his research Waller came across information about a certain lawsuit involving a local man named James Ashton, who had long been deceased. Waller's interest was piqued when he learned that Ashton, a Tacoma land speculator and entrepreneur at the turn of the 20th century, had received a favorable ruling in the 1904 case *U.S. v. Ashton* from Judge Cornelius Hanford concerning the Tribe's right to ownership of land on the Tacoma Tideflats. The judge ruled against the Puyallup Tribe in favor of Ashton. Judge Hanford and Ashton were business partners at the time, so Hanford's ruling brought up a serious question concern-

Puyallup Tribal Council listens to comments from Representative Norm Dicks. (Left to right along table on right): Frank Wright, Roleen Hargrove, Lena Landry, Bill Sterud and Connie McCloud. Courtesy of the Puyallup Tribe.

ing conflict of interest. The judge was later impeached for doing these and other such favors. Since *U.S. v. Ashton* had not been heard by an unbiased judge, it was the smoking gun the Tribe had been searching for. The case tied together information gathered by both generations of the tribal researchers who together set the foundation for the Tribe's coming legal arguments. For 80 years the Tribe had been deprived of those lands because of the ruling and they wanted the case reheard.

The next step was to head to court. In 1980 the Tribe filed an action against the Port of Tacoma to quiet title on approximately 12.5 acres of former riverbed land once covered by the Puyallup River before the U.S. Army Corps of Engineers relocated the river from its original channel in the late 1940s. This left the former riverbed as uplands, which the Port of Tacoma laid claim to. In July 1981, U.S. District Court Judge Jack Tanner ruled that the Tribe had title to this land. The Ninth Circuit Court of Appeals upheld his decision. Port officials drew up an appeal, but in February 1984 the U.S. Supreme Court refused to hear it.

The secured 12.5 acres wasn't all of the land the Tribe laid claim to, and Tribal leaders formed a strategy to address this. The Tribal Council appointed a committee of Tribal members to begin addressing the pros and cons of moving forward into court.

Frank Wright, Jr., then Puyallup Tribal Council chairman, sent a letter to U.S. Representative Norm Dicks, Tacoma Mayor Doug Sutherland, and other political leaders proposing negotiations over other parcels. Negotiations soon ensued, with the Tribe and its legal team led by attorney John Bell on the one side, and on the other side a negotiating team made up of nearly 70 people including representatives of local municipalities, local civic leaders, U.S. Congressmen, private property owners, and representatives of railroads and title insurance companies. This was some prime real estate being debated—the acreage included the section where the Port of Tacoma headquarters is located. This was also where shipping giant Sea-Land wanted a terminal so it could relocate from Seattle to Tacoma. Much of the future development in downtown Tacoma and on the nearby Tideflats depended on settling who had rightful title to the land once and for all, including which governmental entity, tribal or otherwise, would control zoning, police, courts and taxing within the disputed property.

The matter was made more complicated because the boundaries of the Puyallup reservation had been changed from what was originally spelled out in the Medicine Creek Treaty. After the treaty was ratified, Congress split the reservation into allotments granted to Tribal members, but by the early 1900s most of the titles had passed from Tribal members to non-Indians.

In September 1985 an agreement in principle was reached between the non-Indian negotiators and the Puyallup Tribe. It was valued at $112 million, with $27 million of this set aside for removal of a bridge over the Blair Waterway. The remaining money was allocated for trust funds and loan funds for the Tribe, and for a range of social and economic development programs. On Feb. 8, 1986, the Tribe rejected it by a vote of 236 to 158. There were numerous reasons why Tribal members voted against this settlement. Some said the amount didn't come near to being equal to the value of the land. Others said taking money would amount to selling out.

After the vote the non-Indian negotiating team started showing signs of weakening in its commitment to seeing the issue through, but persevered, as did the Tribal members. The Bureau

Puyallup Tribal Council hears from Congressman Norm Dicks. (Left to right): Lena Landry, Bill Sterud and Connie McCloud. Courtesy of the Puyallup Tribe.

of Indian Affairs provided the Tribe with $100,000 for voter outreach efforts.

More negotiations ensued, with people on both sides hoping to avoid litigation. In July 1988 a tentative accord was reached and presented to the Tribal membership for a vote to approve or reject. In this offer there was more for individual tribal members, notably a cash payout, and there were more guarantees about land being put back into trust status, as it had been a century before.

On Aug. 27 it passed with a vote of 319 to 162. By the agreement: 900 acres would be returned to the Tribe; a per-capita payment would be paid to each adult member upon reaching 21 years of age; a permanent trust fund of $24 million would be established for members as well as a fisheries enhancement program, job training and placement program; a small business development fund would be established; social and health service improvements would be made to address the need for an elder care facility and a day care center; and the Blair Navigation Project.

Most importantly, the Tribe got some of its land back. While it didn't regain complete ownership of the 18,000 acres with the reservation, the Tribe did get several parcels ideal for economic development. The settlement paved the way for a boom in international trade at the Port of Tacoma and for much of the development on the Tideflats over the next 20 years. It assured Sea-Land's move to Tacoma and made the South Sound more attractive to the shipping industry. It led to new opportunities for the Tribe, including an agreement with Stevedoring Services of America to build two shipping terminals on Tribal land along Blair Waterway, a $300 million, privately funded port development. Other valuable land includes parcels along the Hylebos

Waterway, home to the Tribe's Chinook Landing Marina, and along the east side of the Blair Waterway, where the Emerald Queen Riverboat would open in 1997.

A permanent trust board and a board of directors (Puyallup International, Inc.) were appointed to oversee the implementation of these projects. Both boards have fiduciary responsibilities to the Puyallup Tribal membership. The trust board is charged with overseeing $22 million held in trust by the United States for the benefit of the Tribe to secure a permanent resource in providing services to the members. Only income earned from the trust may be spent, and only on these programs: housing, elderly needs, burial and cemetery maintenance, education and cultural preservation, supplemental health care, day care, and other social services.

The Puyallup Tribe of Indians incorporated Puyallup International, Inc. (PII), on August 24, 1989 to charter subordinate organizations for economic purposes. In 2007 its board of directors was reorganized and the name changed to Marine View Ventures (MVV). MVV continues PII's work as the economic development arm of the Tribe to create economic opportunities for the Tribe and protect the membership from economic turmoil. MVV controls all non-gaming business ventures for the Tribe, keeping focused on long-term visions to build an asset base that generates significant, stable, and sustainable dividends for the Tribe. MVV is not just profit-driven; the entity seeks to bring returns for the Tribe in employment opportunities, projects like habitat restoration, and land acquisition to expand the Tribe's land holdings through strategic investments to preserve land for future generations.

Although MVV is a business entity that operates separately from the Tribal governing body, it remains an agency and instrumentality of the Tribe. As a separate corporate body, MVV is able to develop, manage, and operate businesses as well as attract new business ventures to the reservation. MVV is also able to invest assets in order to broaden the economic base of the Tribe.

MVV owns and operates three Shell gas stations in Tacoma and the Chinook Landing Marina, one of the premier marinas in the Puget Sound region. MVV also leases property to Ole & Charlie's Marina. MVV's real estate portfolio totals approximately 300+ acres. The portfolio consists of commercial real estate, industrial/port real estate, marinas, gas stations, and billboards. MVV manages these assets under a master lease agreement with the Puyallup Tribe of Indians. MVV is committed to reacquiring lands within the Puyallup Reservation. Reservation land is a finite resource and the significant growth of the region is driving fierce competition for local property. MVV's objective is to expand its land holdings through strategic investments to preserve land for future generations.

Prior to the Land Claims Settlement, relations between the Puyallup Tribal government and its neighboring governments were often tense and antagonistic. After the settlement, the once-impoverished Tribe flourished and became a major player in local and state economics and politics. Things have improved drastically for the Puyallup Tribe in the two decades since the settlement, and the Tribe and local governments haven't faced off in a courtroom since.

THUNDERBIRD AND THE PUYALLUP PEOPLE

Thunder used to come to Kelly's Marsh, east of Sumner, where the women were digging fern roots. Thunder would seize the women, kill them and eat them.

Five brothers resolved, "We will watch for him." The five brothers took bow and arrow and spear. They fought with Thunder for five days; the eldest brother on the first day, the next brother on the second day, and so on until all five brothers had fought.

Thunder became so sick that he said, "Leave me alone and let me live. You shall be my children. You shall go into war and not be killed."

Thunder went away and the people of that place were turned to human beings.

"Tales of Southern Puget Sound"
Arthur Ballard

CHAPTER 10

SELF-DETERMINATION OF THE PUYALLUP TRIBE OF INDIANS

After more than a century of strife among the Puyallup Tribe at the hands of white settlers, Tribal leaders began to regain control of their rights and their future.

The late 1960s through the early 1970s was a time when minority groups fought for their civil rights nationwide, and the Puyallup Tribe was no different. First it was the fishing rights struggles that garnered media attention and caught the eyes and ears of people from outside of the tribal world. In 1976 it was the occupation and takeover of the state-run Cascadia Diagnostics Center, formally a designated Indian hospital, which furthered the message that the Tribe was a force to be reckoned with.

The Tribe began losing their reputation of helpless, second-class citizens, as they had been so wrongly labeled for decades, since as far back as the signing of the Medicine Creek Treaty. After years of being disregarded, lied to and let down by the federal government, tribal leaders had had enough. They began working for themselves, and in a matter of years reasserted their treaty rights and took control of their own welfare. They started with health care and education as a way to benefit individual Tribal members, who would in turn grow and begin to work together as a healthy, educated body, bringing the Puyallup Tribe to where they are today.

Today the Puyallup Tribe is one of the most successful tribes in the country. They own and operate their own education and health-care systems—both deeply rooted in Indian culture and open to members of all tribes in the local vicinity. The Tribe provides some housing for its people, social services, law enforcement, and has a continuing plan for economic development.

But it was not always like that.

At the time of the signing of the Medicine Creek Treaty in 1854, members of the Puyallup Tribe lived entirely off the land. In exchange for moving onto a pre-determined parcel of land, the treaty promised the Tribe the right to fish (which was asserted in the fishing struggles throughout the 1950s and 1960s), health care for all and education for their youth. In 1930 the Bureau of Indian Affairs built Cushman Indian Hospital, which at the time was considered to be the best-equipped hospital in Tacoma, and the largest Indian hospital in the country.

Over time the hospital became designated as a tuberculosis-only treatment center, drastically cutting general health services for Native Americans in the area. In 1959 the hospital was completely shut down, leaving an immense void in the treaty's guarantee to provide health care to members of the Puyallup Tribe.

Following the closure of Cushman, the Tribe was assured that full medical services would still be available through the "Contract Healthcare Program." Implementation was underfunded and programming was ambiguous to patients and pro-

Cushman Hospital employees prepare their float for the Washington State Daffodil Festival's Grand Floral Parade. Courtesy of the Puyallup Tribe.

Scenes from the Washington State Daffodil Festival. Courtesy Ione Knox Collection.

viders, and in general did not lead to good medical care when contract services were used.

According to an account by the Puyallup Tribe's physician in 1976, problems with the contract care services led to only episodic care for Tribal members. For instance, as late as the 1970s the majority of Indian births were to mothers who came to the emergency room in labor with no prior pre-natal care.

Dental care was provided to the Tribe through a mobile-dental van which visited the Tribal cemetery parking lot once a year. Tribal members would wait in lines outside the van only to witness their friends and relatives filing out of the other end in pain and torment from their often painful procedures.

During that time, when Puyallup Tribal members experienced a severe lack of health care and medical attention, the average life expectancy was 45 years for Native Americans, compared to 70 years for other U.S. citizens. The infant mortality rate was almost one and a half times the national average.

Education prior to the creation of the Tribe's own school consisted of white-assimilation boarding schools during the early century, where children were taken from their homes and prohibited from practicing their Native language and culture. When the public school system grew to be sufficient in the 1940s, boarding school students were then shuffled into their prospective neighborhood schools, and most dropped out during high school if they made it that far.

It became clear to the Tribal Council in the early 1970s that in order to grow and prosper as a Tribe, its members would need to be healthy and educated. High dropout rates as well as high infant mortality and disease rates would continue to keep the Tribe from realizing its potential as a self-sufficient government, and even more so as a key player in the local economy.

In 1975 the federal government issued the Indian Self-determination Act, which allowed federally recognized tribes to have more control over starting and running their own entities, such as a health clinics and schools. Tribal leaders, specifically Chairwoman Ramona Bennett and council members Maiselle Bridges, Silas Cross, and Don Matheson, began tireless efforts to lobby the federal government for funds. In 1974 the Tribe applied for Title 4 funding through Indian Education and acquired the Hawthorne School, which was a surplus building, from the Tacoma Public School District. The Tribe rented the building for $1 a year and began to offer daycare services, a counseling and tutoring center for youth and adult education training for early childhood education in a partnership with Fort Steilacoom College.

"Our leadership was looking at the needs of the people... we needed to look at education of the membership, the staff—for our families, our communities, our children. That was the foundation."
Peggy McCloud, tribal member

Acquiring the Hawthorne School building for social services was a start, but Tribal leaders continued to lobby the federal government for money to build a full school for the youth and a clinic for the membership. Many youth arrived at Hawthorne with little to no educational background, or had dropped out at young ages, and it was clear that the Tribe needed its own school. The Bureau of Indian Affairs continued to deny the Tribe funds. Eventually the Puyallup Tribe acquired money through the Self-Determination Act for the first Chief Leschi School. They also received self-determination funds for a clinic

Tribal Council Members ca. 1970: From left: Bill Sterud, Silas Cross, Jr., Don Matheson and Frank Wright. Courtesy of the Puyallup Tribe.

Puyallup Tribal Council June 2006. From left: Lawrence LaPointe, Henry John, Frank Bean, Kathy Lopez, Bill Sterud, David Bean and Herman Dillon, Sr. Courtesy of the Puyallup Tribe.

shortly thereafter.

As one of the first tribes at the time to go after the self-determination money, they were able to establish for themselves one of the first Indian-run "self-determination clinics" and "self-determination schools" in the country. The clinic started out of a triple-wide trailer located between the Cushman Cemetery and the Cushman Building in 1976. The first Chief Leschi School was located in the same vicinity. The Tribe was able to use the money from the Act to build a small school for the elementary school students, located about where the Emerald Queen Casino tent structure is currently. Junior high and high school students occupied parts of the Cushman building. The daycare moved from the Hawthorne School in 1975 into the basement of the Indian Fellowship Church, which was located adjacent to the cemetery as well. In each of its entities—the school, the clinic, and the daycare—the Tribe was able to re-incorporate language and culture into its teachings and practices, an aspect of the Puyallup culture that had been squelched and concealed for more than a century.

The relocated daycare was named Orenda, which is the name for the female spirit in the Seneca Nation's language. It served about 50 youth for two years. The Chief Leschi Junior High and High School was held in the Cushman building until it was condemned in 1991; then the upper-level students were relocated to Saint Anne's Catholic School campus in South Tacoma. The clinic operated out of the trailer for close to 20 years, serving a population of thousands of Native Americans from tribes throughout the region. Modular units were used for the dental procedures. The modular units, set up in 1976, were temporary and intended to be operational for only five years, but they held the clinic and its services for close to 20 years. Tribal leaders worked tirelessly to appropriate more money from Congress for a larger, permanent structure, but for many years requests were ignored.

In the 1990s leaders began seeking additional federal BIA funds for the clinic and the school to create permanent, reliable structures to accommodate growth and increasing needs. In 1993 the Tribe opened its current medical clinic Takopid. At the time the $8 million facility was expected to serve the 7,000 patients who used the clinic. It was the largest tribally run medical center in the Pacific Northwest. In 2009 it was one of only two tribally run clinics in the Northwest Indian Health Services region that serves Native American descendents outside of the host tribe's affiliation. Indian Health Services funded the 36,000-foot facility, which coupled state-of-the-art technology with traditional healing practices. The clinic houses medical and dental services, a pharmacy, community health programs, a dental laboratory, and x-ray facilities. It added 25 staff positions when it opened in 1993, and gave health-care providers the additional space needed to serve the population.

In the 1980s the clinic added a drug and alcohol treatment center, offering inpatient and outpatient counseling services to clients with substance abuse issues. In 2009 the treatment center restructured, closing down the inpatient portion in order to offer more youth treatment options.

In 1999 the Kwawachee Counseling Center was added to the Takopid umbrella. The state-of-the-art mental health facility offered youth and adult counseling services, case management, and family therapy. Like all aspects of the Puyallup Tribal Health Authority, Kwawachee Counseling Center incorporates traditional healing practices and spiritual well-being into its patient care and employee relations. The methods are the fusion of many traditions including a "Long Horse Tradition" of an unidentified northern Puget Sound group, the pipe ceremony of the Plains region, the sweat lodge, Shaker traditions, and Plains sage incense therapy.

In 2009 the Health Authority employed a staff of more than 200 well-trained professionals and technicians. They consistently provide nationally accredited health care to an active patient population exceeding 8,500.

In 2008 fiscal year, the Health Authority spent $25 million providing health care. Of the $25 million, $12.5 million was spent on the health clinic, $1.4 million on alcohol and drug treatment, $369 thousand on community health, $2 million on mental health, and $308 thousand on diabetes treatment.

In 1985 the Health Authority became a Joint Commission of Accreditation Healthcare Organization. In 2009 the clinic received its diabetes accreditation, giving it the tools to offer full diabetes education and care to the population with a high risk of diabetes. Convincing the federal government of the Tribe's need to receive funding for a new school was even more of an ordeal than securing money for the Takopid clinic.

Puyallup Tribal Council member Rolleen Hargrove traveled back and forth from Washington, D.C. working closely with Congressman Norm Dicks and Senator Daniel Inouye before finally receiving funds and developing plans in the early 1990s. By 1996 the school was constructed and opened for education for enrolled tribal students in the area. Now all students preschool through grade 12 were located in the one central location. The state accredited 200,000-square-foot private school has become a model for Native American programs around the country and shows a glimpse into the future of educational technology for all educators.

Chief Leschi School serves Native American students from more than 60 different tribes with current enrollment of approximately 890 students who attend pre-kindergarten through 12th grade. Additional early childhood education was added through the construction of the Grandview Early Learning Center in 1996, which was originally built to accommodate Puyallup parents who were working or who were in school, as Grandview stayed open until late in the evening. Now Grandview is a full-service educational center for children from birth to school age, and also is a daycare center for school-aged children after school up to age 12. In 2008 the Tribe allocated $1.8 million for daycare services to Tribal members, and Grandview served 100 children on a daily basis.

Northwest Indian College, based out of the Lummi Reservation in northern Washington state, ran a branch campus on the Puyallup reservation until 1993. The Tribe did not renew its licensing for the school and created their own tribally run college in 1993. The Puyallup Tribe's Medicine Creek College started by offering five classes in partnership with Pierce College in the tribal administration building on Portland Avenue. When the program began in 1993 there were 30 students. That number doubled by the second year. The college focused on law enforcement, business, education, mental health and alcoholism counseling, tribal business management, and a vocational-based office professional program. It also offered general equivalency diploma preparation. In 1997 the college, which became the only Native American tribal college in the south Puget Sound, graduated its first class. The Medicine Creek Tribal College closed its doors after 1999.

After the closure of the college, the Tribe continued to invest in human capital by spending millions of dollars each year on

Map showing the Puyallup Tribe's plans for its land holdings at Port of Tacoma. Courtesy of the Puyallup Tribe.

education of youth and adults. In the 2008 fiscal year, the Tribe spent $17.8 million on education, which included $14.2 million for Chief Leschi School. The remaining $3.4 million was dedicated to educational assistance including college tuition, books and living assistance for enrolled Puyallups seeking higher education. The Tribe assisted 200 tribal members attending college in 2008. The Tribe also spends close to $1 million on an Education Incentive Program, which encourages enrolled Puyallups to obtain and maintain good grades throughout their school years.

ELDERS CENTER

In 2008 the Tribe took steps to honor their elders by breaking ground on an Elders Center that had been more than 20 years in the making. During the late 1980s, the Tribal Council obtained architectural services for the schematic design. A lack of funding prevented the project from proceeding for several years.

In 2006 the Planning and Land Services department hosted a series of community meetings seeking input from the elders as to what features they would like in the center. Council reserved funds for the $10 million center in 2007 for the facility, and fully funded the design and construction of the project. During the planning and design stages of the facility, Elders Services operated out of the old Polish Hall on East 30th Street near Portland Avenue in Tacoma.

The site for the new 26,000-square-foot facility was selected at Duct Cho for its proximity to the tribal administration building and the health clinic, and the availability of trust lands. The new facility is a state-of-the-art-health, wellness, and community center built specifically with the elders' needs and desires in mind. It was appropriately labeled House of Respect.

An outdoor spirit garden, spa, and wellness center, community gathering space, banquet room, library, art, and indoor and outdoor activity space is all afforded in the Elders Center. A 12,00-square-foot vegetated roof reduces storm water run-off, absorbs carbon dioxide and increases oxygen. It is a symbol of the Tribe's connection to the environment and the outdoors. The Elders Center opened in October 2009.

PUYALLUP TRIBAL NEWS

In July 1989 the Puyallup Tribe received a voice for itself, and started the *Puyallup Tribal News* as way to open communication among the membership and the surrounding public. Prior to the inception of the *Puyallup Tribal News*, tribal member Prudy Matheson independently created a small newsletter for distribution among Tribal members, which included birth announcements, birthdays, deaths, and personal news of Tribal members for Tribal members. Prior to the development of the paper, there was little in the way of published communication for the Puyallup Tribe.

During the controversial times of the Land Claims Settlement, the Tribe needed a way to express their side of the story that had been skewed by the mainstream media for years. Through the newly established paper and public information office, the Tribe was able to be fully represented in mainstream media, which had been lacking during many controversial stories surrounding the self-determination of the Tribe. The Tribe was able to begin educating the public and media about such issues as tribal sovereignty, which started to clear up misconceptions. The average reader didn't fully understand the Tribe's rights, and therefore didn't understand the issues and steps the Tribe took to regain many of those rights. This played a key role in the strengthening of inter-jurisdictional relationships that the Tribe continued to develop into the 21st century. The paper was also a tool to communicate tribal issues and new developments to the membership.

The paper received a lot of attention starting out, and in its first year received three awards at the Native American Journalist Convention, which was held on the Puyallup Reservation in 1990. In 2002 the *Puyallup Tribal News* was contracted out through Pierce County Community Newspaper group, which published suburban, community-focused papers throughout Pierce County. In 2006, the paper switched from a monthly to a bi-weekly product to expand communication between the council and the membership. It is dispersed at tribal buildings and locations throughout the reservation, and mailed to every enrolled Puyallup Tribal member in the country to create maximum communication.

CHAPTER 11

FINANCIAL SELF-DETERMINATION/ CASINOS

With the Puyallup Indian Tribe having won back an important portion of its tribal lands as a result of the Land Claims Settlement of 1988, the Tribe turned its attention to making use of this newly secured property on Tacoma's growing waterfront. Situated on the Blair Waterway among the hustle and bustle of the Port of Tacoma, the valuable acreage provided a choice urban location for the Tribe to launch its biggest economic venture ever—a luxurious new casino that would quickly propel the once impoverished Tribe to new heights of success.

Initially opinions of the local public differed on whether it was a good thing to bring gambling to the Tacoma area for the first time. Some people had moral objections, while others expressed fears of organized crime and general seediness. However, the multimillion dollar casino proved to be a hit, largely because of its novel location—on an authentic paddlewheel riverboat, christened the "Emerald Queen," moored right on the water for guests to board and enjoy all kinds of table games, beverages, and entertainment. All decked out like an expensive hotel with plush carpets, chandeliers, natural light, cozy sitting areas, and antique furniture, its three-day grand opening in the spring of 1997 was a real celebration with fireworks, laser shows, and live bands.

Just a few miles off busy Interstate 5, the casino's waterway home, situated in a high-traffic corridor, was perfect for attracting tourists. Locals came by the busload as well, and business boomed. An Emerald Queen Casino companion location, in the old Puyallup Bingo Hall just miles from the riverboat, also attracted big crowds and had to be expanded with a temporary addition.

But the EQC meant more than a swanky new place to have fun; it provided another firm step for the Puyallup Tribe on its road of self-determination. The casino's success reached beyond the reservation in numerous ways, including providing nearly 1,000 full-benefit jobs for workers in the area. The casino soon became one of the biggest employers in Pierce County and enjoyed a fine reputation for actively supporting local resources. The EQC used all local vendors, secured financing through a local bank, and contracted with all local firms for construction and maintenance. Moreover, the Tribe invested revenue generated from the casino in local communities, and income earned by its employees was spent within the local community as well. This set a precedent from which the Tribe has never wavered— to use its gaming earnings for the betterment of Puyallup tribal members first, then for communities at large. Over the decades, profits from the EQC have been regularly turned right back to the tribal members, opening up opportunities to establish social services, help the elderly and children, and basically make life

The Tribe's very first casino opened in 1997 in an authentic riverboat parked along Tacoma's growing waterfront. The land addition was added later. Courtesy of the Puyallup Tribe.

better for the embattled Tribe.

Less than ten years after opening for business, the EQC was thrown a curve ball. Officials at the Port of Tacoma announced plans to open a new container port for shipping giant Evergreen Shipping Agency on the Blair Waterway. To do so, the main road to the casino would have to be closed. Tribal attorneys pointed out that such a closure would have an immediate, and negative, impact on the casino, as revenues would certainly fall drastically and many jobs would be sorely threatened. In addition, the Tribe had also set up its tribal government and administrative offices in a building just up from the riverboat, so more concern developed among tribal leaders over access to the Tribe's headquarters.

On top of all this, there was a definite deadline the port had to meet in order to keep its new contract with Evergreen or risk ruining the deal, a deadline set to arrive within months of the Tribe being notified of the port's intent. This put the Tribe in a real time crunch to find a new casino location, and quickly. There were legal issues to consider as well in making such a move. At that time the state would only approve casino sites located on trust lands. While there were numerous properties on the Puyallup reservation ideal for a gaming facility, there were no properties in trust that were large enough, much less at a location with as much accessibility to the public as could be had on the I-5 corridor.

The Puyallups were presented with a dilemma: to either legally challenge the Port's plan to close the road in order to buy time while the fed's long, drawn-out process of putting land into trust status plodded along, or convince the state to change its rule and let the Tribe open a casino on the reservation right away, and then start the trust status process on the property.

Above all, tribal attorneys made it clear that no move would be made without equitable relief for the Tribe.

A coalition formed to address the matter, made up of tribal representatives and counsel, representatives from the state, the City of Tacoma and Pierce County government, and signatories to the land settlement agreementv of 1988, which included the City of Puyallup. The Tribe had a federal congressional delegation backing them up, including some powerful Republicans that saw the logic in the Tribe's quest to change the state's regulation.

This was an historic moment for the Puyallup Tribe, one that would be forever etched in its legacy when the announcement came: the state would allow for a new EQC to be established where the Puyallups wanted it to be rather than be restricted to trust lands only. The Tribe purchased a Best Western Hotel and Conference Center just off I-5 in Fife and got to work modifying it to have it fully operational before the road closure to the riverboat. The Puyallup Tribe's governmental and administrative offices secured a comfortable home as well in Tacoma where they remain today in the heart of the reservation.

In November 2005 the new Emerald Queen Casino and Hotel opened in Fife. Together with its additional location in Tacoma, the EQC resumed its place as a bedrock business in South Puget Sound and one of the most consistently successful casinos in the Northwest.

With such successful gaming operations, the Tribe was able to launch a per-capita payment program for its membership, which allowed enrolled tribal members to improve their quality of life and invest in big purchases like homes and cars. The casinos provide a slew of living-wage jobs, training and educational opportunities, and provide benefits for communities and neighboring governments. State law requires tribes that operate casinos to provide a minimum of two percent of the net win on table games to local jurisdictions to mitigate the impact of gaming facilities. The Puyallup Tribe provides funds each year to the cities of Tacoma, Fife and Puyallup, Pierce County and the state of Washington. Since the original EQC opened in 1997, the Tribe has provided millions of dollars to fund road projects, law enforcement, court operations, fire and medical response and other services. As a result, the Tribe and its neighboring governments have developed strong working relationships. Between 1997 and 2006, overall spending by all facets of the Tribe, including the casinos, went from $49.6 million in 1997 to $284.49 million in 2006, for a total of $1.573 billion during the casinos' first decade of operation.

The EQC provides monies for a Charitable Trust Fund that donates money to local charities like the Ronald McDonald Foundation, American Cancer Society, March of Dimes, Tacoma Rescue Mission and Mary Bridge Children's Foundation, among many others. The trust fund board of directors has one half of one percent of the casino's table game revenue to disperse, which averages to about $1 million each year in community donations. The board receives thousands of requests each year and determines recipients based on their community service and non-profit status.

The EQC also sponsors community events like Taste of Tacoma and "Zoobilee," the Point Defiance Zoo and Aquarium's annual fundraising gala. In 2008 the Puyallup Tribe granted $685,000 to the zoo, the largest donation in the zoo's history.

The Puyallup Tribe of Indians has made great strides in improving the lives of its members and boosting the local economy ever since the Tribe ratified the historic Land Claims

Settlement in 1988. The future looks very bright for the Puyallup Tribe's "entertainment capital of the Northwest," as the EQC continues to live up to this reputation. The EQC Showroom remains a favorite performance venue for big names in popular music of all varieties, along with stand-up comedians from HBO and Comedy Central, and title boxing tournaments aired on ESPN and HBO. Gaming at both EQC locations continues day and night. The Emerald Queen Casino I-5 offers 56 favorite Vegas-style table games like Blackjack, Craps and Roulette, and over 2,000 video slot machines. Machine gaming is the specialty at Emerald Queen Hotel & Casino with over 1,490 video slots and a large variety of classic table games.

Those looking for a fine dining experience can find it at both EQC locations. At the Emerald Queen Hotel & Casino in Fife, the Tatoosh Grill offers an intimate atmosphere and a panoramic view of Mount Rainier as guests dine on haute cuisine featuring the world's finest natural Angus beef, wild seafood and authentic Chinese cuisine. The Pacific Rim Buffet features prime rib, sushi, cook-to-order pasta, and an array of desserts. The Emerald Queen Casino I-5 in Tacoma, guests can choose from the International Restaurant's menu of gourmet Chinese, American and continental cuisine. The International Buffet offers American and Asian dishes, plus a Surf & Turf Buffet with all you can eat crab legs. The Asian Garden Café features fresh spring rolls, Saigon crepes, char-grilled meats and a selection of exotic soup and noodle dishes. The Palace Deli has traditional offerings such as pizza, burgers, espresso, and pastries. All ages are welcome at the EQC restaurants.

CHAPTER 12

TRIBAL ORGANIZATION TODAY

Through efforts of self-sufficiency and determination in recent decades, the Puyallup Tribe has been able to emerge from its struggles as a strong, incredibly generous entity. The Tribe was able to reach and surpass many of its cultural, social, and economic goals and is continuously living up to its reputation of "generous and welcoming behavior to all people."

In 2008, the Tribe donated over $5 million to various charities. Through their Charity Fund and Community Impact contributions, the Tribe provided $3.4 million to local governments, schools, churches, and various non-profit organizations supporting food banks, children's literacy programs, medical research, education and job training, to name a few.

In addition to the Charity Fund and Community Impact contributions required by the Tribe's Gaming Compact, the Tribe also contributed $1.6 million to various governments and non-profit organizations in 2008. Specifically, the Tribe donated $425,000 to the City of Fife for a swimming pool renovation, $100,000 to Tacoma Firefighters for renovating a fireboat, $100,000 to the Tacoma Public Schools as part of a 5-year funding commitment and $100,000 to Mary Bridge Children's Foundation, along with donations to numerous other organizations.

The Puyallup Tribe puts the future of its members and their abilities to further their educations at the forefront of their priorities and is constantly searching for new ways to reward achievement.

School-aged children are able to receive help with costs associated with sports teams, band, extracurricular activities, and driver's education. Member focus on school and good grades is rewarded with the Educational Incentives Program, which was founded to encourage tribal member children, youth, and adults to work diligently in bringing up and maintaining good grades, to attend school regularly and to improve their academic performance, thereby increasing their knowledge, skills and abilities to succeed in post-secondary educational institutions. These types of reward programs help ensure that future adults in the Puyallup Tribe will be on the right path toward leading the next generation.

The Tribe's Higher Education Program provides tribal members with financial aid to assist high school graduates and adults continuing their education with the rising costs associated with pursuing a higher education. This program allows students to further their knowledge and better their careers and continue the tradition of excellence and generosity embedded in the Tribe.

The Tribe puts a significant emphasis on the investment of human capital. During 2008, the Tribe spent $17.6 million on education for its youth and adults. Of the $17.6 million, $14.2 million was spent by Chief Leschi Schools Inc., a chartered corporation of the Puyallup Tribe. The purpose of the school is to provide education for pre-kindergarten through 12th grade Native American students. Approximately 728 students were in enrolled in 2008.

The remaining $3.4 million was spent on providing Tribal members with educational assistance. During 2008, the Tribe assisted 200 Tribal members through funding of $1 million on tuition assistance and $500,000 on books and living assistance. Lastly, the Tribe spent over $900,000 on the Education Incentive Program.

Continued health, medical assistance, and disease prevention is another essential facet of the Puyallup Tribe's dedication to its members. The Puyallup Tribal Health Authority (PTHA or health authority) was established in the early 1970s in response to a lack of consistent quality health care available to the Puyallup Tribe of Indians and all other Native Americans residing in Pierce County. As one of the first Indian self-determination clinics, the Tribe's medical clinic has grown from a mobile home to occupying modern, attractive and culturally designed buildings. The staff of over 200 well-trained professionals and technicians provides nationally accredited health care to an active patient population exceeding 8,500.

During the 2008 year, the Health Authority spent $25 million providing health care. Of the $25 million, $12.5 million was spent on the health clinic, $1.4 million on alcohol and drug treatment, $369,000 on community health, $2 million on mental health and $308,000 on diabetes treatment.

The Puyallup Tribe remains conscientiously proactive on urban issues that have been tied to Native American individuals such as substance abuse. The Community and Family Services program provides assistance to Puyallup tribal youth and adults who need drug and alcohol screening, assessments and referrals to treatment services, which all focus on intervention, prevention and outreach services to the Native American community on or near the Puyallup reservation. Counseling, family support, and other financial assistance are all available to tribal members who need it and are trying to get their lives back on track.

The Puyallup Tribal Housing Authority is an essential aspect of the Tribe and its abilities to assist members. The housing authority's mission is to provide assistance and opportunities for eligible and qualified Native Americans within the Puyallup Tribe's service area to obtain affordable and sufficient housing.

The housing authority has been established to provide decent, safe, and sanitary housing for low-income tribal members and other Natives; to remedy unsafe and unsanitary housing conditions that are injurious to the public health, safety, and morals; to alleviate the acute shortage of decent, safe, and sanitary dwellings for persons of low income; to provide employment opportunities through the construction, reconstruction, improvement, extension, alteration or repair and operation of eligible dwellings; and to manage and maintain residential properties that are owned by the Tribe and/or the housing authority for the purpose of providing housing to Tribal members and the Indian community. Puyallup Tribal Housing Authority offers assistance to eligible low-income participants with rental assistance, low rent housing, home-ownership opportunities and the repair and renovations to homes owned by elders.

Land planning and community development are imperative to the Tribe's continued efforts to flourish and thrive and acquire property to expand their services to members. This department is primarily responsible for Tribal community planning, real estate and Trust services, intergovernmental project coordination, property acquisitions, land use and building permits, land planning and GIS services, and the coordination of facilities planning within the reservation. Also responsible for managing the land-use planning and consultation obligations of the Tribe as described in the Land Settlement Agreement of 1989.

The mission of the Puyallup Tribe's land planning and community development departments is to develop and implement a responsive land use planning and land management program that will protect, preserve and enhance the fishery, natural, cultural, economic, and land resources of the Tribe within the reservation for the benefit of its members, their families and future tribal generations.

The Puyallup Tribe achieved a great many feats in terms of land planning and development during the 2008 year including coordinating the presentation of community meetings to get member input for the design and development of community facilities: the Elder Center and community/youth center; conducting over six major mailouts and questionnaires to the membership on preferred facilities and their locations; Casino relocation options on Portland Avenue area, and Justice Center site concepts for Council review and planning purposes; coordinating the purchase of over sixty (60) properties within the Portland Avenue area and other areas within the reservation.

In 2008, the Puyallup Tribe spent $3.6 million on natural resource protection. Key departments include water quality, air quality, wildlife, fisheries, and environmental. These departments have implemented environmental codes, air quality regulations, water regulations, and coordinated endangered species recovery and restoration projects for rebuilding off-channel habitat projects. In addition, the Tribe's fisheries department completed its 12th annual Puyallup River watershed salmon, steelhead, and char spawning report. This report presents the most detailed review of anadromous (salt water to fresh water) fish distribution and abundance available.

All of the Puyallup Tribe's efforts to support its members ultimately fall under the all-encompassing purpose—retaining cultural resources for future generations to experience and continuing to hold events that celebrate members who have made gains for the Tribe in the past. The Tribe spent $1.2 million on Cultural Resource Protection in 2008. These funds were allocated to the Tribe's Historic Preservation Department, the Language Preservation program, and the annual Canoe Journey and Labor Day Pow-Wow event. The Historic Preservation Department educates the tribal and non-tribal community about the history and culture of the Puyallup Tribe of Indians. It ensures that sacred lands are protected from growing development by requiring that outside agencies consult with the Tribe before a project commences on Tribal lands and/or any of the Tribe's usual and accustomed areas.

The Puyallup Tribe continues to use its means to benefit its members, neighboring tribes, and the surrounding community. The furthering of education to its youth and adult members, preservation of health and wellness in the Tribe, support of neighboring cities and organizations, and the development of land acquisitions such as the Emerald Queen Casino at Fife expansion will only further serve to affirm the Tribe as a vital, essential, successful community in the South Puget Sound.

Staff of the Puyallup Tribal Health Authority (PTHA). Courtesy of the Puyallup Tribe.

BIBLIOGRAPHY

CHAPTER 1 – BEFORE THE SETTLERS CAME

Shackleford, Elizabeth. "The History of the Puyallup Indian Reservation." Bachelor's thesis, College of Puget Sound. 1918.

Smith, Marian. The Puyallup-Nisqually. New York: Columbia University Press, 1940.

Smith, Marian. "The Puyallup of Washington" in Acculturation of Seven Indian Tribes. Ed. Ralph Linton. New York: Appleton Century Company, 1949.

Smith, Marian. "Coast Salish of Puget Sound." American Anthropologist, 43. 1941.

Historic Preservation Office, Puyallup Tribe of Indians. "Tribal History Remembered" (John "Xot" Hote). Puyallup Tribal News. Pg. 3. Oct. 4, 2007.

Bick, Marguerite, Ed. National Lawyers Guild Law Student Indian Summer Project Report. Seattle, 1973.

CHAPTER 2 – EXPLORERS AND SETTLERS ARRIVE

Ruby, Robert H. and Brown, John A. "A Guide to the Indian Tribes of the Pacific Northwest." University of Oklahoma Press: Norman and London, 1986.

Eckrom, J.A. "Remembered Drums: A History of the Puget Sound Indian War." Pioneer Press Books: Walla Walla, 1989. George Pierre Castille, ed. "The Indians of Puget Sound: The Notebooks of Myron Eells." University of Washington Press: Seattle and London, 1985

American Friends Service Committee. "Uncommon Controversy." Before the Treaties. pgs. 8-17

"Spanish Exploration: Juan Perez Expedition of 1774 – First European Discovery and Exploration of Washington State Coast and Nueva Galicia (the Pacific Northwest." History Link. www.historylink.org/index.cfm?DisplayPage=pf_output.cfm&file_id=5677

Ed. Murray C. Morgan. "Peter Puget on Puget's Sound." Puget's Sound: A Narrative of Early Tacoma and the Southern Sound. University of Washington Press, 1979. p. 4-14.

Rochester, Junius. "Vancouver, George." History Link. March 4, 2003. www.historylink.org/index.cfm?DisplayPage=output.cfm&file_id=5359 Accessed March 28, 2009.

Becker, Paula. "Meeker, Ezra (1830-1928)." HistoryLink.org. May 2, 2006. www.historylink.org/index.cfm?DisplayPage=output.cfm&File_Id=7737. Accessed March 31, 2009.

Ed. Clifford E. Trafzer. "Indians, Superintendents, and Councils: Northwestern Indian Policy, 1850-1855." University Press of America, Inc.: Lanham, Md., 1986.

Wilma, David. "Michael T. Simmons settles at Tumwater in October 1845." January 22, 2003. www.historylink.org/index.cfm?DisplayPage=output.cfm&file_id=5089. Accessed March 31, 2009.

Carpenter, Cecelia Svinth. "Fort Nisqually: A Documented History of Indian and British Interaction." Tahoma Research Service, Tacoma: 1986.

"School History." Chief Leschi Schools. www.leschischools.org/about/history.php Accessed: April 21, 2009.

CHAPTER 3 – MEDICINE CREEK TREATY

Lange, Greg. "Smallpox epidemic ravages Native Americans

on the Northwest Coast on North America in the 1700s." Jan. 23, 2003. www.historylink.org/index.cfm?DisplayPage=output.cfm&file_id=5100

Richards, Kent. D. <u>Isaac I. Stevens: Young Man in a Hurry</u>. Washington State University. December, 1993.

Ruby, Robert H. and Brown, John A. <u>Myron Eells and the Puget Sound Indians</u>. Seattle: Superior Publishing Company. 1976.

Reddick, SuAnn M. and Collins, Cary C. "Medicine Creek to Fox Island: Cadastral Scams and Contested Domains." www.historycooperative.org. Oregon Historical Quarterly 106.3 (2005). www.historycooperative.org/journals/ohq/106.3/reddick.html.

Letters from Special Agent Wesley B. Gosnell to Isaac Stevens, circa 1856.

Smith, Marian. <u>The Puyallup-Nisqually</u>. New York: Columbia University Press, 1940.

"The Donation Land Claim Act, 1850." (full text) www.ccrh.org. Center for Columbian River History. www.ccrh.org/comm/cottage/primary/claim.htm.

"Native American tribal leaders and Territorial Gov. Stevens sign treaty at Medicine Creek on December 26, 1854." www.historylink.org. www.historylink.org/index.cfm?DisplayPage=output.cfm&file_id=5254.

"Puget Sound Business Directory and Guide to Washington Territory." Compilers and Publishers: Murphy & Harned, Olympia. 1872.

"Indian Jim was true: A warm tribute from one who knew him thoroughly." <u>Tacoma Daily Ledger</u>. Pg. 3. June 30, 1890.

"A Monograph on the Puyallup Indians: A Plea for the Puyallups". Prepared for Congress by A. Boston Tilicum, Esq. Tacoma, Wash. 1892.

Wickersham, James. "The Indian Side of the Puget Sound Indian War." Oct. 30, 1893.

Correspondence letter to Hon. D.M Browning, Commissioner of Indian Affairs, Washington, D.C. from Commissioners James J. Anderson, John W. Renfroe and Ross J. Alexander. Tacoma, Wash.: Dec. 21, 1893.

"Puyallup (tribe.)" www.wikipedia.org. http://en.wikipedia.org/wiki/Puyallup_(tribe).

Tacoma Daily Ledger. "Will give away $2000 at potlatch in honor of dead." June 20, 1907.

"A Puyallup Puzzle." Tacoma Ledger. Feb. 6, 1894.

"Indian Killed by Interurban." Tacoma Ledger. April 2, 1905. Sworn testimony of Joseph Dick. State of Washington, County of Pierce. Feb. 3, 1905.

Washington State Board of Health Burial Permit for Albert Kautz. April 29, 1914.

Sworn testimony of Pierce County Coroner Conrad L. Hoska for Tommy Thomas. April 4, 1900.

Sworn testimony of Peter John, son of John Salerhanul. Dept. of the Interior, U.S. Indian Service. State of Washington, County of Mason. May 29, 1899.

CHAPTER 4 – EDUCATION AND HEALTH OF FAMILIES AND CHILDREN

Sicade, Henry. "Henry Sicade's History of the Puyallup Indian

School, 1860 to 1920." Columbia Magazine. Ed. Cary C. Collins. Winter 2000-2001, Vol. 14, No. 4.

Sicade, Henry. "The Cushman Indian School: A Brief History, 1927." Tacoma Public Library Northwest Room. Catalogue number: NWR 970.3 S11.
Collins, Cary C., Ed. "Henry Sicade's History of Puyallup Indian School, 1860-1920." http://wshs.org. http://wshs.org/wshs/columbia/articles/0400-al.htm.

Olsen, Winnifred L. Tacoma Beginnings: The First 100 Years. Tacoma Public Schools. 1969.

Marr, Carolyn J. "Assimilation Through Education: Indian Boarding Schools in the Pacific Northwest." http://content.lib.washington.edu/aipnw/marr.html. Accessed March 18, 2009.

"Henry Sicade." Fife High School. http://www.fifeschools.com/fhs/history/sicade.html. Accessed May 11, 2007.

Caster, Dick. "Father Hylebos, St. George's Indian School and Cemetery, and St. Claire's Mission Church." Historical Society of Federal Way. October 15, 2003. www.federalwayhistory.org/Articles/FtHylebos.PDF. Accessed March 18, 2009.

"About Us: American Lake." United States Department of Veterans Affairs. November 20, 2008. www.va.gov/puget-sound/page.cfm?pg=13. Accessed March 30, 2009.

Interview: Judy Wright, Puyallup Tribal Historian.

CHAPTER 5 – GOVERNMENTAL ORGANIZATION OF THE TRIBE

Hunt, Herbert. History of Tacoma. Chicago: S.J. Clarke Publishing Company. 1916.

Wheeler Howard Act (Document).

Constitutions and Bylaws of the Puyallup Tribe of Indians Dicynebt.

Indian Reorganization Act (Document).

Interviews with Puyallup Tribal Attorney John Bell.

History, City of Puyallup. www.cityofpuyallup.org. http://cityofpuyallup.org/visitors/history.

History, City of Edgewood. http://72.11.68.141 http://72.11.68.141/CityInfo/history.htm.

CHAPTER 6 – FISHING RIGHTS STRUGGLE

American Friends Service Committee. <u>An Uncommon Controversy: Fishing Rights of the Muckleshoot, Puyallup, and Nisqually Indians</u>. University of Washington Press, 1970.

"Our People." www.theolympian.com. http://news.theolympian.com/150th/96249.shtml.

"Biography – Dick Gregory for the people." www.dickgregory.com. www.dickgregory.com/dick/about_dick_gregory.html.

"The World According to Dick Gregory: An Evening of Humor and Humanity." www.sphinxmg.com. http://sphinxmg.com/artist/dick-gregory-2.

"Dick Gregory begins hunger strike in Olympia jail on June 6, 1968." www.historylink.org. www.historylink.org/index.cfm?DisplayPage=output.cfm&file_id=5462.

"Dick Gregory is hospitalized on the 39th day of his hunger strike on July 4, 1968." www.historylink.org. http:www.historylink.org/index.cfm?DisplayPage=output.cfm&file_id=5464.

Dick Gregory is released from Olympia jail under house arrest on July 16, 1968. www.historylink.org. www.historylink.org/index.cfm?DisplayPage=output.cfm&file_id=5465.

Cummings, Robert. "Tanner asks pardon for Dick Gregory." The News Tribune. June 13, 1968.

"Gregory's release sought by attorney." The News Tribune. July 16, 1968.

"Dick Gregory 'satisfactory' in hospital." The News Tribune. July 5, 1968.

Smith, A. Robert. "Court hears Indian fish arguments." Tacoma News Tribune. March 26, 1968.

Bailey, John. "Six jailed in Olympia fish protest." Tacoma News Tribune. Sept. 9, 1968.

Nelson, Dale. "1968 Nisqually fishing case before high court Monday." Tacoma News Tribune. May 24, 1970.

"BIA upholds Indian Puyallup Control." Tacoma News Tribune. August 14, 1971.

Lane, Bob. "White – Indian: What's back of fish fight." Tacoma News Tribune. August 26, 1971.

"Ruling termed 'racist': High court says Satiacum guilty, reserve [reservation – ed.] defunct." Tacoma News Tribune. April 13, 1972.

Lane, Bob. "6 Indians arrested in Nisqually sweep." The News Tribune. Jan. 4, 1972.

"4 Indian civil suits dismissed." Seattle Post-Intelligencer. June 24, 1972.

"Hank Adams sets surrender time." *Tacoma News Tribune*. Jan. 12, 1972.

Mayne, Jack. "Game Dept. kept dossiers on Indians, says Adams." *Seattle Post-Intelligencer*. Sept. 4, 1973."

"The Indian fishing war in pictures." *The News Tribune*. Nov. 19, 1973.

Ryan, Jack. "Defiant Indians fish the Nisqually again." *Seattle Post-Intelligencer*. Feb. 24, 1973.

Mottram, Robert. "Did Indians turn to farm?" *Tacoma News Tribune*. Sept. 9, 1973.

Wilkins, Jack. "Expert asked for 'fair share' fish plan." *The News Tribune*. Sept. 4, 1973.

Wilkins, Jack. "Indian fishing suit delay effort fails." *The News Tribune*. August 25, 1973.

Ryan, Jack. "Indians, state still at odds on fishing." *Seattle Post-Intelligencer*. Feb. 21, 1973.

"Indians seize state game headquarters." *Seattle Post-Intelligencer*. Jan. 29, 1973.

"Indian-game unit confrontation near." *The News Tribune*. Jan. 29, 1974.

Mottram, Robert. "Against fish ruling: 700 sportsmen stage protest." *The News Tribune*. March 5, 1974.

Nesvig, Jonathan. "Judge Boldt says he's proud of abuse received." *The News Tribune*. Feb. 5, 1975.

"Indians to catch steelies despite chum salmon ban." *The News Tribune*. Feb. 7, 1976.

"Puyallup Tribe cited by state game department." <u>Tacoma Indian News</u>. Vol. 1, No. 5. Jan. 13, 1977.

Nelson, Sandy. "Janet McCloud: Fishing rights battle drew Tulalip woman onto the front lines." <u>The News Tribune</u>. Jan. 30, 1984.

Campobasso, Melissa. "Maiselle Bridges: Matriarch of treaty rights." <u>Puyallup Tribal News</u>. Pg. 3. May, 1996.

Currier, Erika. "Wright went fishing to give tribes the right." <u>Puyallup Tribal News</u>. Pg. 9. Nov. 1998.

Tizon, Alex. "25 years after the Boldt Decision: The fish tale that changed history." www.seattletimes.com. Feb. 7, 1999. www.kohary.com/env/bill_020799.html.

Bell, John. "The Tribe's battle over treaty fishing rights." <u>Puyallup Tribal News</u>. Pg. 13. March, 2000.

Bell, John. "The long battle for the right to fish for steelhead." <u>Puyallup Tribal News</u>. Pg. 17. April, 2000.

Gottfriedson, Allison. "Remembering the fishing struggles." <u>Puyallup Tribal News</u>. Pg. 12. March, 2000.

Wilma, David. "United States Department of Justice sues the state of Washington over treaty fishing rights on September 18, 1970." www.historylink.org. August 25, 2000. www.historylink.org/index.cfm?DisplayPage=output.cfm&file_id=2626.

"Tribal rights activist McCloud dies at 69." <u>www.spokesmanreview.com</u> (Spokane, Wash.) Nov. 28, 2003. www.spokesmanreview.com/allstories-news-story.asp?date=112803&ID=s1447255.

Crowley, Walt and Wilma, David. "Federal Judge George

Boldt issues historic ruling affirming Native American treaty fishing rights on February 12, 1974." www.historylink.org. Feb. 23, 2003. http://historylink.org/index.cfm?DisplayPage=output.cfm&file_id=5282.

Dodge, John. "Years After the Boldt Decision: Ruling reshaped fishing, tribal rights - Echoes of landmark case linger." The Olympian. Feb. 9, 2004. www.citizenreviewonline.org. www.citizenreviewonline.org/feb2004/years.htm.

Marritz, Robert. O. "Billy Frank, Jr. (b. 1931)." www.historylink.org. March 10, 2009. www.historylink.org/index.cfm?DisplayPage=output.cfm&file_id=8929.

"Boldt Decision." www.wikipedia.com. June 18, 2010. http://en.wikipedia.org/wiki/Boldt_Decision.

Frank, Jr. Billy. "Boldt brought management to state." Northwest Indian Fisheries Commission. www.nwifc.org. www.nwifc.org/2004/03/boldt-brought-management-to-state.

Kamb, Lewis. "Boldt Decision 'very much alive' 30 years later." www.seattlepi.com www.seattlepi.com/local/160345_boldt12.html.

CHAPTER 7 – CASCADIA TAKEOVER

"Violence averted in Indian Takeover." (Editorial) Tacoma News Tribune. Nov. 3, 1976.

Shomshak, Vern. "Superintendent agrees: Cascadia handled with care." The News Tribune. Nov. 2, 1976.

Gille, John. "Is it Cascadia, Cushman or Chief Leschi?" Tacoma News Tribune. Oct. 31, 1976.

"Armed Puyallup Indians blockade Cascadia." The News Tribune. Nov. 2, 1976.

O'Connor, Paul. "The Takeover: Indians win – and lose too." Seattle Post-Intelligencer. Oct. 31, 1976.

"Indians leaving Cascadia, plan school, medical center." The Seattle Times. Oct. 31, 1976.

Mottram, Robert H. "Indians dance as drums laud possible agreement." The News Tribune. Oct. 25, 1976.

Mottram, Robert H. "Cascadia 'treaty' satisfies Indians." The News Tribune. Oct. 31, 1976.

Jones, Marjorie. "Institutions for juvenile offenders to be closed." The Seattle Times. June 15, 1979.

Pugnetti, Jerry. "Cascadia wins round; bid to hike WSH funding fails." The News Tribune. March 21, 1979.

Red Swallow, Riva with Riley, Rick. "20 year struggle ends: Cushman returned." Tacoma Indian News. Vol. 4 No. 8. June 27, 1980.

Jenkins, Pat. "Cascadia rent talks dragging on." The Seattle Times. July 5, 1980.

Weathersby, Jeff. "Tribal decision on plans for Cascadia expected soon." The News Tribune. June 19, 1980.

Zahler, Richard and Strick, Stan. "State asks ruling against Indians." The Seattle Times. June 13, 1980.

Turner, Joe. "State diverting juveniles from Cascadia." The News Tribune. June 16, 1980.

Jones, Marjorie. "Indians plan for Cascadia transfer." The Seattle Times. June 19, 1980.

Jones, Marjorie. "State, Indians to discuss Cascadia transfer to tribe." The Seattle Times. June 20, 1980.

"State may sue feds over loss of Cascadia." The News Tribune. June 23, 1980.

King, Warren and Brooks, Tom. "Indians, state ease tensions over Cascadia." The Seattle Times. June 15, 1980.

Jones, Marjorie. "Puyallup Nation prospering at former juvenile center." The Seattle Times. Nov. 3, 1981.

"Indians plan trade center at Cascadia." Pierce County Herald. Jan. 20, 1981.

Miller, Margaret. "Hard Road On 'Indian Path' – Puyallup Finds Tribal Heritage." www.seattletimes.nwsource.com http://community.seattletimes.nwsource.com/archive/?date=19930517&slug=1701735. May 16, 1993.

Deaderick, Sam. "Tribe evicts state from Cascadia Center." Puyallup Tribal News. Oct. 1994.

Bell, John Howard. "Tribe's fighting spirit reflected in building's history." Puyallup Tribal News. Sept. 1999.

Currier, Erika. "Membership votes to take down admin building." Puyallup Tribal News. Vol. 12 No. 7. July/August 2001.

CHAPTER 8 – TRIBAL LAW ENFORCEMENT

Interview: Daniel Duenas, Sr., Chief of Police, Puyallup Tribal Police Department. May 2009.

CHAPTER 9 – LAND CLAIMS SETTLEMENT OF 1988

Shatzkin, Kate. "A New Future? Reading Between the Lines of the Puyallup Settlement." The Seattle Times. http://seattletimes.nwsource.com. http://community.seattletimes.nwsource.com/archive/?date=19900225&slug=1058033 Feb. 25, 1990.

Larson, John. "Land Claims Settlement: 20 Years Later." Puyallup Tribal News. Issue No. 71. Sept. 18, 2008.

Larson, John. "Land Claims Settlement Celebrated." Tacoma Weekly. Sept. 25, 2008.

CHAPTER 10 – SELF-DETERMINATION OF THE TRIBE

Gordon, Susan. "Building their own success: Expectations are exceeded at the new Chief Leschi, now a model school in American Indian education." The News Tribune. P. B-1. June 12, 1997.

Maynard, Steve. "Northwest Indian college moves and another school takes shape." The News Tribune. p. B2. Sep 27, 1993.

"Puyallups' medical center opens with technology and tradition." The Associated Press. Seattle Post-Intelligencer. P. B2. Sept. 14, 1993.

CHAPTER 11 – FINANCIAL SELF-DETERMINATION

Carson, Rob. "Casino to open Friday: Puyallup Tribe's $10 million gambling venture in Tacoma eventually will include a 292-foot riverboat." The News Tribune. Dec. 26, 1996.

Barber, Mike. "Wheels Turning in Puyallup Casino." Seattle Post-Intelligencer. April 18, 1997.

Carson, Rob. "A Riverboat Gamble: Puyallups are betting big with a casino different from the others." The News Tribune. April 13, 1997.

CHAPTER 12 – TRIBAL ORGANIZATION TODAY

"Port, Tribe make deal on terminal development," by Meghan

Erkkinen. <u>Puyallup Tribal News</u>. Feb. 21, 2008. www.puyalluptribalnews.net/article/220.

"Port, tribe sign historic agreement," by Meghan Erkkinen. <u>Tacoma Weekly</u>. April 24, 2008. www.tacomaweekly.com/article/1876.

Interview, David Bean, tribal council member.

Interview, Bill Sterud, tribal council member.

Interview Tara Mattina, port spokesperson.